BACKGROUND·TO·
English-speaking Countries

RICHARD MUSMAN

MACMILLAN
PUBLISHERS

ACKNOWLEDGEMENTS

The publishers and author wish to acknowledge with thanks the following sources of extracts and illustrations, and to state that they have made every effort to trace all copyright holders. If they have failed to do so, they will be pleased to make the necessary adjustments at the first opportunity.

Edward Arnold for an extract from *Languages of Britain* by Glanville Price
Cambridge University Press for extracts from various editions of *English Today*
The Daily Telegraph for an extract from the Peterborough Column
The Economist Publications for statistics from *The World in Figures*
Newlands Knight and Round Ltd, 33 Bruton St, London W1 for the New Zealand advertisement
Pergamon Books for an extract from an article by Fred Tempes (*EFL Gazette*, November 1985)
UNESCO for data from the *UNESCO Statistical Yearbook* 1984 (c) UNESCO 1984
F A Hoyos for an extract from *Barbados Our Island Home* (Macmillan)

Illustrations
Australian Information Service: plate 12
Barnaby's Picture Library: pp 89, 90, 95, 97
Jon Beck: maps and p 139
Ann Bolt: p 110
Bury St Edmunds Information Service (West Stow Village): plate 2
Camera Press: pp 13, 48, 123
Canadian Government Information Service: plates 8, 9
J Allan Cash: p 102
Colorsport: pp 120, 141
Robert Harding Associates: plate 14
Ralph Harrington: pp 20, 47, 75
G W Lennox: plate 13, pp 19, 112, 115, 116, 118
Mansell Collection: pp 80, 107, 130, 135
Kate Mattock: pp 99, 101
Museum of Modern Art, New York: p 41
National Army Museum: p 56
New Zealand Information Service: plate 11; pp 84, 86
Rex Parry: plates 16, 17, 18, 19; pp 140, 146
Popperfoto: p 36
Arthur Ridley: p 81
Josie Wall: plates 1, 5; p 67

All other photographs are the copyright of the author.

Contents

Contents

First published 1987
Reprinted 1990 (twice), 1993

Published by MACMILLAN PUBLISHERS LTD
London and Basingstoke

Printed in China

Musman, Richard
    Background to English-speaking Countries.
    1. Commonwealth of nations
    2. United States
    I. Title
    909.0975210828   DA10.5

ISBN 0-333-41598-1

English is the most widespread language on earth and is second only to Mandarin Chinese in the number of people who speak it.

"Outside Britain. . . a number of third world Englishes are evolving to join the older Englishes in Britain, America, Australia and elsewhere."

Tony Fairman, *English Today 7*, July 86

English is the most widely used 'lingua franca' in the world. When Europeans meet Japanese, when Indians meet Nigerians, when Brazilians meet Malaysians, they are likely to discuss their business in English. Inside great countries like India there are many different languages. The most common Indian language is Hindi, but the large population of Tamils in southern India find it easier to learn English than Hindi. So Indians from the north usually speak English when they meet Tamils.

Approximate figures

World population	4.7000,000,000 people
People speaking English as a first language	325,000,000
People who often use English as an extra language	300,000,000 (some experts say 1,000,000,000)

The English – speaking world

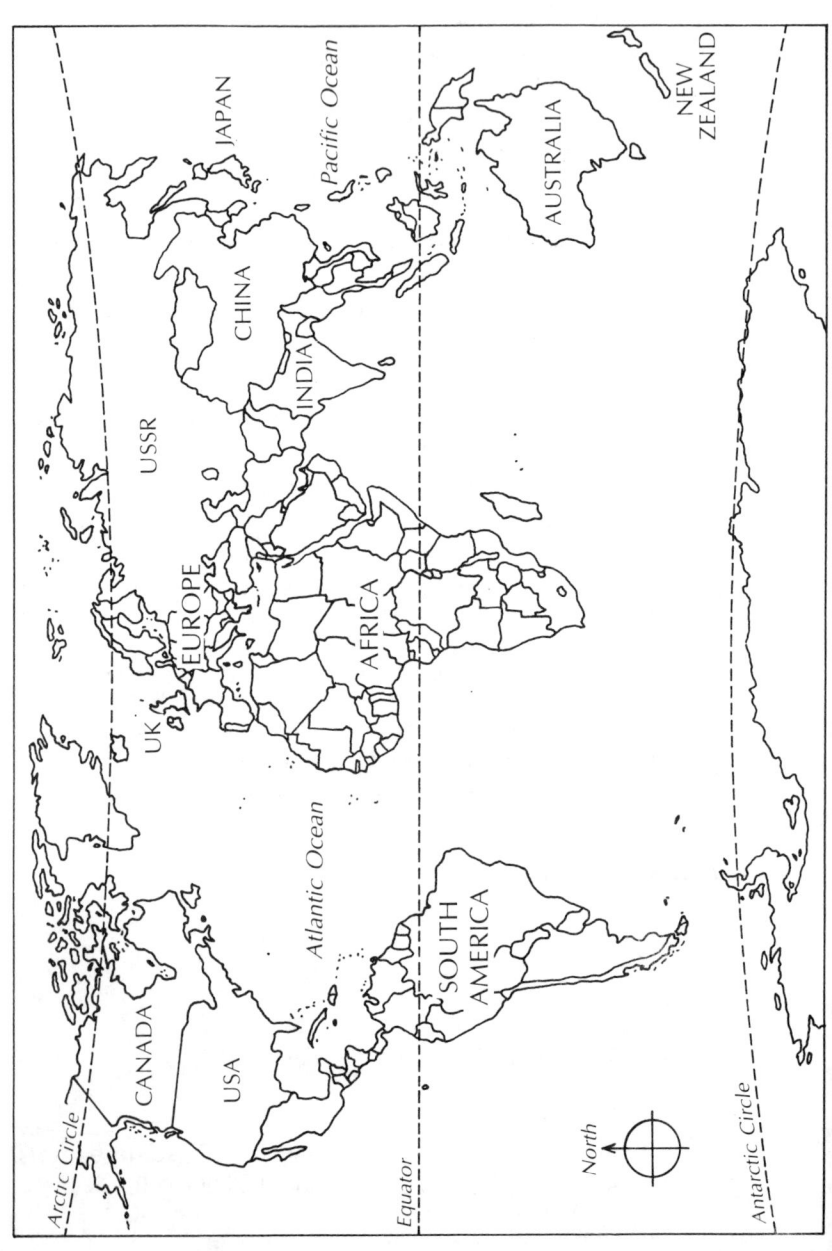

♦ the official language, or one of the official languages, in a multi-language country—used in Parliament, business, colleges, etc.

♠ not the official language, but an important extra language in countries once part of the British Empire

AE American English

Africa

West Africa and southern Africa

♦Gambia
♦Sierra Leone
♦Ghana
♦Nigeria
AE ♦Liberia
♦South Africa (English and Afrikaans)
♦Namibia—South African dependency (English and Afrikaans)
♦Botswana
♦Lesotho
♦Swaziland

East Africa

♦Kenya (English and Swahili)
♦Tanzania (Swahili and English)
♦Zimbabwe
♦Uganda
♦Malawi

North Africa

♦Sudan

Pacific

◊Australia
◊New Zealand
♦Fiji, Tonga, Samoa, Solomon Islands, Gilbert Islands, Ellis Islands

Asia

◆India (English and Hindi)
◆Pakistan (English and Urdu)
◇Sri Lanka (Silhala)
◇Bangladesh (Bengali)
◇Malaysia (Malay, Chinese and Indian languages)
◆Singapore (English, Chinese, Tamil)
◆Hong Kong (English, Chinese)
AE ◆Philippines (English and Pilipino)
◆Seychelles
◆Mauritius

South America and islands of the South Atlantic

◇Guyana
◇Falkland Islands
◇Saint Helena
◇Ascension Island
◇Tristan da Cunha

Central America and Caribbean

◇Antigua, Bahamas, Barbados, Belize, Bermuda, Cayman Islands, Jamaica, Saint Vincent, Trinidad and Tobago
◆Saint Lucia, (English and mixed English and French dialect)
◆Puerto Rico (English and Spanish)

North America

◆Canada (English and French)
AE ◇USA

Europe

◇UK
◇Eire (English and Irish Gaelic—but many more speak English than Gaelic)
◆Gibraltar (still a British colony)
◆Malta (English and Maltese)

UK

1 Who are the British?

'GB' on the back of British cars abroad is short for Great Britain, which is the name for England, Scotland and Wales. 'The UK' is short for the United Kingdom of Great Britain and Northern Ireland. However, most people call the UK 'Britain', and many foreigners simply say 'England', which is incorrect and particularly annoys the Scots.

The Scots, Welsh and Irish are Celts, but the English are Anglo-Saxons. The Scots are prouder of being Scottish than British and they are proud of their names. One and a half million Scottish names in Britain begin with M', Mc or Mac, which means 'son of' in Gaelic, the old Celtic language of the Scots. The publisher of this book has a Scottish name. Welsh names are quite different. Names beginning with 'Ll' are Welsh, like Llewellyn and the first name, Llyn. Other common Welsh names you will find in the telephone book, wherever you go in Britain, are Lewis, Davies, Morgan, Edwards.

The names of most English people, too, come from their ancestors*, the Germanic Angles and Saxons, who invaded* Britain in the fifth century AD. The commonest English name is Smith, which, like the German name, Schmidt, means 'a worker in metal'. Some English families have Norman French names which go back to the Norman Conquest of 1066: D'Arcy, Beaufort, Beauchamp (pronounced 'Beecham'). But for centuries there have been marriages between Anglo-Saxons, Celts and Normans. John Smith could have more Celtic or Norman blood in him than Anglo-Saxon.

> There are about 800,000 people called Smith in England and Wales, and about 1,700,000 in the USA.

The ancestors of the Welsh were the Ancient Britons, who escaped from the invading Angles and Saxons and found shelter in the wild mountains of Wales. The Welsh defended their freedom for 1000 years and were not conquered by the English until 1536. However, the modern Welsh keep alive their past. The people who live in the hills and valleys still

---

*ancestor your great-great-great-great grandfather/mother etc.
invade to enter another country using force

speak their ancient Celtic language. In fact, about a quarter of the Welsh nation still speak Welsh as their first language, though nearly all of them also speak perfect English. Throughout the year they have festivals of song and dance and poetry called *Eisteddfodau,* and on these occasions many of them wear Welsh costumes. The great event of the year is the National Eisteddfod. It is so popular that there is not a hotel room free for miles around. The big moment of this Eisteddfod is the poetry competition and the giving of the prize to the winner. The Welsh are great rivals of the English and they show their fiery patriotism* at rugby matches against England. Before the match they sing their national song, *Mae Hen Wlas Fy Nhadan (Land of Our Fathers).* The band no longer plays *God Save the Queen,* because some of the Welsh crowd called it the English national song, and they used to shout and whistle.

'Of all the languages spoken at the present time in mainland Britain, Welsh has been here by far the longest.'

Glanville Price *Languages of Britain* (Edward Arnold 1985)

Some Germanic Angles settled in the Scottish lowlands and in the borderlands between Scotland and England, but they never invaded the Highlands, where the Scots remained safe in their mountain glens and on their islands. Scots still love to remind Englishmen that they destroyed the English army at the Battle of Bannockburn in 1314, and they are proud that the English never conquered them. The union of the two countries in 1707 took place by agreement between them. The Scots have their own Church, the Presbyterian Church of Scotland. Strict Presbyterians believe there should be no work or pleasure on the Lord's Day (Sunday). But times are changing. There are still elderly Presbyterians who spend Sunday reading the Bible, but pubs now open on

*patriotism love of your country

Sunday and good Scottish Presbyterians drink their 'wee dram of Scotch' (little drop of whisky) after church. Only about 80,000 Highlanders still speak Gaelic.

> 'Seeing Scotland, Madam, is only seeing a worse England'.
>
> Samuel Johnson, 1778

Three centuries ago Scots and English Protestants were sent to live in Northern Ireland. It was hoped that they would help to stop the Irish Catholics from causing trouble. When English armies came to Ireland to fight the rebellious Irish, the Northern Ireland Protestants fought on the side of the English. Every year they remind the Catholics of their victories by marching through the streets of Belfast and Londonderry with drums, and waving flags. Since 1922 Eire has been independent.

The killings in Northern Ireland today are the result of this history. The most fanatical Protestants will never agree to share any power with the Catholics who form a third of the population. The terrorist group, the IRA (Irish Republican Army), which claims it is 'protecting' the Catholics in Northern Ireland, wants a united Ireland run by themselves. Many IRA members are not Catholics. Some are Marxists. The British Government and the Government of Eire are now working together to bring peace to Northern Ireland. Both governments, as well as the Catholic Church, are against any form of violence. There are also Protestant terrorist groups.

The terrible potato famine of 1845–6 in Southern Ireland left behind an undying hatred of the British. In all parts of the world there are still Irish people who cannot forgive the British for letting more than a million die of starvation.

Many of the black people you meet in any British city today are 'second generation' British citizens with local accents like Cockney (London) or 'Brum' (Birmingham). Since the Second World War, West Indians, Indians, Pakistanis, have been coming to Britain to find work and to escape the terrible poverty in their homelands. It has not been easy for them to find decent jobs or decent places to live. There are laws to protect them from unfair treatment, but these laws do not always work successfully. Most of the non-whites in Britain are British citizens and they now form about 4% of the population.

A Scotsman's Scottishness increases with his distance from Scotland

6   Who are the British?

A   Vocabulary

1   What is the opposite of *incorrect*?
2   What is the meaning of *conquest*?
3   Name something which is made of *metal*.
4   On what occasions do people look for *shelter*?
5   Find another way of saying *keep alive the past*.
6   What is the difference between *Scotch* and *Scottish*?

B   Questions

1   What is the difference between the United Kingdom and Great Britain?
2   What is the meaning of the name *Macdonald*?
3   What happened at the Battle of Bannockburn?
4   What is the differenct between the ancestors of Smith and Beauchamp?
5   What do the Welsh do at an Eisteddfod?
6   What do the Protestants do in Belfast and Londonderry every year?
7   Why did West Indians and Asians come to Britain?

C   Further Information — Grammar

Using the following passage, ask questions about John Bull.

Example.

Is John Bull really a typical Englishman? Is he really a quiet fellow? Does his face. . . ?

John Bull (typical Englishman) was once a rather a quiet fellow. His face never showed what he was feeling, because both school and parents had taught him to 'keep a stiff upper lip'. His mouth must not turn up to show enjoyment or down to show sorrow, even if his best friend died. Of course he never cried. Jane Bull was very like her husband. They were fond of one another, but they hid their feelings.
    The British today are no longer afraid of showing their feelings.

D Function

Like/dislike

I/They like/don't like/quite like — I/They love/hate — I/They enjoy/don't enjoy — It's/They're terrific/awful/all right/fairly nice — I/They approve/don't approve

Choose the right phrase to fill in the gaps below.

Friend What do you think of your own country?
You   ...
Friend Do you like your own name?
You   ...
Friend How do you feel about learning English?
You   ...
Friend Do you approve of violence?
You   ...
Friend Why do some people read poetry?
You   Because...
Friend What do the Welsh think when they beat the English at rugby?
You   ...

A Pakistani butcher's shop in London

2 The UK government and how the British vote

THE QUEEN Head of Government, but she is a constitutional monarch (which means she governs through Parliament).

PARLIAMENT House of Commons (635 elected members); House of Lords (Dukes, Lords, Peeresses, etc, the Archbishops of Canterbury and York and 24 senior Bishops). Both Houses debate and vote on bills introduced by ministers. It is the vote of the House of Commons that counts. The House of Lords can make changes in bills. When passed, bills become Acts of Parliament, which eventually become law.

PRIME MINISTER Leader of the Party which forms the government (gets the most seats in a general election— Margaret Thatcher 1983).

CABINET Council of about 30 ministers chosen by the Prime Minister.

CIVIL SERVICE Permanent non-party political administrators* who run government departments, eg Foreign Office, Home Office, etc. They advise ministers and carry out their policies.

The United Kingdom is not a federation. The Scots have charge of their own education, police, housing and agriculture* and they have their own legal system*, but not their own Assembly. Northern Ireland once had its own Parliament for local affairs, but will go on being governed from Westminster so long as violence continues. Wales has a nationalist party, *Plaid Cymru* (Welsh for 'Party of Wales', pronounced 'Plide Cumry'), but in a referendum in 1979 the Welsh voted against a separate Assembly. So did the Scots.

Britain has a form of democratic government which has grown over the centuries and is made up of hundreds of Acts of Parliament. This constitution, as it is called, has gradually taken away more and more power from the monarch, so that today the King or Queen has no political power. But the British people love the Royal Family, who are much more free and easy than they used to be. They walk among the crowds and talk to people with humour and real interest.

*administrator person who runs a government or business office
agriculture farming
legal system the way the laws of a country are dealt with

All bills passed by Parliament must be signed by the monarch, however much he or she may dislike them, and today when Queen Elizabeth opens Parliament, wearing her crown and all her glittering regalia*, the speech she reads out is not her own, but the Prime Minister's, even though she uses the first person, 'I' throughout.

The UK is divided into 635 constituencies (areas which are represented by a Member of Parliament). The three main parties are Conservative, Labour and Alliance (a coalition between the Liberal Party and the new Social Democratic Party, SDP, who broke away from Labour in 1981).

Let us imagine that the people of Brigham, a market town near London, are about to vote in a general election. For generations Brigham has always been a Conservative seat, and the voters are mostly retired couples, tradesmen, middle-class commuters*, farmers and the self-employed. But now many people are changing their minds, especially the unemployed and those with low incomes. They don't like Labour, but they are also losing their faith in the Conservatives, so they may try the Alliance, which seems ready to make changes without being too left-wing. They like the Alliance candidate, Sue Newcombe. She's young, bright and intelligent and when she argues, she gives as good as she gets, but never loses her temper.

'Don't be fooled by that pretty face!' Sir Roland Royce, the Conservative candidate warns. 'Sue Newcombe is a charming woman, but would you really like to have her as your representative in Parliament? She's had no experience of managing anything except her Mum's sweet shop. We need

*__regalia__ decorations which the Queen wears on special occasions
__commuter__ person who goes every day from country home to city office

a strong government to deal with the growing violence in our society. The Conservative Party stands for law and order, and we want to show the world that Britain is still great.'

Roger Steward, Labour candidate, laughs at Sir Roland's claims. 'Britain will remain a second-class nation so long as we carry this terrible burden of unemployment and poverty, for which the Conservatives are entirely to blame. Labour want to see that the poor, the sick, the old get all the help our Welfare State has to offer . . . No, madam, we really mean what we say . . . The EEC, sir? We'll hold a referendum to see whether the British people want to stay in or come out . . . Yes, sir, we'll give the Trade Unions all the support we can, and we'll fight for better conditions and better pay for working-class people, but don't, I beg you, be fooled by the Alliance. If you put Sue Newcombe and her fellow candidates into power, you'll fall between two stools. They have no experience of governing. There'll just be a terrible muddle.'

'Just listen to those two!' says Sue Newcombe. 'Labour gives the impression that the only people who need help and support are *working-class* people. What narrow-minded

Leaflets delivered for a Parliamentary candidate before an election

nonsense! Everyone who works belongs to the working class! And Sir Roland still believes that people educated at public and grammar schools are the backbone of Britain. What nonsense! The Alliance is the only classless, non-racist party, and it will also fight for the equality of the sexes. We don't promise to do away with unemployment. That would be unrealistic. But we do promise to reduce it by a million. We are firm believers in the Welfare State. We'll also try to put some 'go' back into the country by introducing a form of profit-sharing. And we'll introduce proportional represent-ation. Isn't it right that a party which wins 30% of the votes should have 30% of the seats? That's what would happen if we had PR. Under the present voting system, it is possible to win 30% of the votes, but gain only 50 seats.'

Sir Roland wins the election, but Sue Newcombe is close behind, losing by only 450 votes. Roger Steward is a long way back in third place, but Labour rarely does well in county constituencies. The Brigham result is a setback for the Conservatives, since Sue Newcombe has reduced their majority there by 6000.

A   Vocabulary

Which goes with which?

referendum	men and women having the same opportunities
retired couples	nothing where it ought to be
burden	natural and not feeling shy
free and easy	she argues just as well as he does
lose one's temper	a national vote for something important
she gives as good as she gets	old people (men and women) no longer working
muddle	heavy load which makes you tired
equality of the sexes	being very angry

B   Questions

1   What did Margaret Thatcher become after the 1983 election?
2   What is the last thing that happens to a bill passed by Parliament?
3   What political party did most of the SDP leave before forming their own party?
4   Brigham has always been a Conservative seat. What does that mean?
5   What did Sue Newcombe say about the word 'working-class?'
6   Why did Labour do badly at Brigham?

C   Grammar

Take the paragraph beginning 'Don't be fooled by . . .' and turn it into reported speech, as if it was a newspaper article.

Sir Roland Royce warned people not to be fooled by a pretty face. He agreed that . . .

D   Function

Making promises

you promised — you gave us your word — you said you would help — you've broken your promises — you agreed

Fill in the gaps in the dialogue with phrases from above.

R. Steward   We have always done much more for old people than the Conservatives.
Elderly Lady   That's not true . . . but . . .
R. Steward   No, madam, we never break our promises.
Lady   . . . to increase our pensions, but you didn't.
R. Steward   We never promised that.
Lady   . . ., but your word doesn't mean anything these days.

R. Steward	How did we break our word?
Lady	. . . to raise old age pensions by 50%.
R. Steward	Oh, no, madam, we never agreed to that.

3   The British worker—wealth from the sea

Bill and John, two university students, were having an argument about the British worker. 'We have too many strikes,' Bill said.

'Miserable wages and high taxation, that's the cause,' John replied.

'Some workers go on strike if one of their mates is fired for doing deliberate damage, or for stealing money. Workers who do that sort of thing deserve to be fired.'

'You mean the management can't do wrong!' John said.

'No, of course I don't mean that,' Bill snapped. 'You seem to think the workers can do no wrong.'

Firemen on strike

'Go inside any big car factory,' John said. 'You'll see that the management is much more worried about production than about the welfare of the workers. Managers treat workers as if they were machines.'

'We have too many unions,' Bill said. 'There are more than 600 in Britain.'

'I don't agree,' John replied. 'Every one of these unions is needed. Some of them are more than 200 years old.'

'That's just what I'm complaining about,' Bill argued. 'They're so old they're no longer needed. Some big factories employ workers who belong to fifteen different unions. Ten men from just one union can close a whole factory if they go on strike. The employer takes a big risk if he fires a worker who is lazy, or arrives late and leaves early.'

John was angry. 'Are you suggesting that the British worker is lazy? If so, you got it out of one of the cheap newspapers.'

'Well, tell me why our shipbuilding yards are getting so few orders these days? . . . It's because they can't deliver on time. They have too many tea-breaks, too many men who take the day off.'

'No!' John cried. 'That's nonsense! Shipbuilders in other countries are having just as difficult a time.'

A report published in 1985 claims that workers and management get on much better than most people think. Britain actually loses fewer days from strikes than the USA and Canada. There are many more small factories, manufacturing anything from pencils to Lotus cars, and in these factories there is a sort of family pride and a readiness to work after hours without claiming overtime (pay for working late). ICI (Imperial Chemical Industries) has never had a strike, because the employees* are given a share in the firm's profits. But unemployment is a serious problem.

Unions, ballots and the police

'One of the best laws passed in the last few years,' Bill began, 'is the law which says there must be a ballot* of all members before there's a strike. Take the miners' strike of 1984/85.'

*employees people who are employed
ballot secret vote

Welsh miners coming from the pit

'No!' John protested. 'It's over, finished. It's not important any more.'

'You're wrong!' Bill cried. 'It was the longest, most bitter strike there's ever been, and a lot of miners didn't want it. Why do you think the Nottingham miners have left the National Union of Mineworkers and formed their own union, the Miners' Democratic Union?'

'The miners would have won the strike if they had all supported the NUM,' John said, 'and if the police hadn't prevented the strikers from stopping the "scabs" going to work.' ("scab" is an insulting word for a man who tries to go to work during a strike.)

'John!' Bill said, 'the law says that striking workers may stand outside a factory and try and *persuade* men not to go to work. It's against the law to block the road or use force. Yet policemen from all over the country were called to the mines to keep the roads open and of course there was violence.'

'Yes,' John said hotly, 'violence by the police!'

'No, by both sides ... I think it's undemocratic to stop men from going to work when they want to.'

'And I,' John replied, 'think it's undemocratic to go against your mates. They were striking because the National Coal Board threatened to close pits* that were running at a loss.'

'Quite right.' Bill commented. 'No worker can expect to be kept on in a business that's running at a loss.'

North Sea oil

In the 1960s oil and natural gas fields were discovered under the North Sea, most of them in the stormy ocean round the Shetland Islands. Now platforms* and drilling rigs* rise above the grey waves, the oil flows through pipelines to a great terminal in the Shetlands. From there it is carried by tankers to every part of the world. The gas, all that the UK needs, flows through pipes from the gas fields to the mainland. There it is odorised* before flowing on to British factories, cookers and gas fires. Without the smell it would be dangerous.

North Sea oil is too light for diesel oil, but perfect for petrol. So the UK sells some of its light oil abroad and, with the money earned, imports heavy oil for factories, locomotives and lorries.

A   Vocabulary

wages — strike — human being — lazy — profit — support — deliver — violent — to close — terminal — fired

Fill in the gaps with the word which fits the sense. There are more words in the above list than you need.

1   He never works hard. He's ...

2   He's a skilful worker, but his ... are lower than mine.

*pits coal mines
platform (here) holds machine which draws oil from oil field
drilling rig makes holes (drills) in sea-bed to look for oil
odorised given a smell

3 He's . . . He's always hitting people.
4 He was . . . because he always arrived at the factory an hour late.
5 A dog is an animal. A factory worker is a . . .
6 His business is doing well. Last year he made a large . . .

B   Questions

1 Why, according to Bill, do some workers deserve to be fired?
2 What can happen if ten important workers from one union go on strike?
3 What was the longest, most bitter strike there's ever been in the UK?
4 According to a report published in 1985, which of these countries loses fewer days from strikes than the others: USA, UK, Canada?
5 What does the law allow striking workers to do outside a factory?
6 But what did striking miners actually do?
7 What fuel do (a) cars (b) lorries/trucks run on?

C   Grammar

Make up short sentences about everyday life, using the tense which is shown in brackets (present perfect, past simple, past perfect)

Example **damage** (Past simple) I damaged my bike.

steal (present perfect)	**keep** (past simple)
think (past simple)	**find** (past perfect)
lose (past simple)	**carry** (past perfect)
stop (present perfect)	**run** (present perfect)

D   Function

Anger or indignation

Read again the passage on strikes. Then make up a dialogue between a striking and a non-striking miner, but remember both sides are angry and are sure they're right. Here are some phrases suggesting anger.

You're talking nonsense. You're just thinking of yourself. You're on the side of the bosses. What do you think unions are for? It'll be your fault. You make me mad!   That's stupid. No, I'm not.

4   The British out of doors

The British spend as much time as they can out of doors, in spite of the weather. Sometimes in summer it is grey and wet for day after day, while in winter it can be sunny and dry and even warm. Families who can afford it, keep ponies, and many people hire horses from riding stables, for riding is very popular, especially among girls. You can go pony trekking (riding long distances with a guide) in the wilder parts of Britain, on Exmoor and Dartmoor in the West Country, and on the hills and mountains of northern England, Scotland and Wales. Pony trekking is one of the best ways of seeing Britain, because there are so many bare hilltops with wonderful views.

> No place in Great Britain is more than 117 kilometres from the sea.

Family holidays by the seaside in towns like Blackpool, Brighton or Scarborough are very English. The children build sand castles on the beach, while their parents dip their feet in the waves or sleep in deck chairs, and the whole family eats shell fish and enjoys all the different amusements on the piers. People who want a quiet seaside holiday go to the unspoilt rocky coasts of Devon and Cornwall, Scotland and Wales.

From spring until autumn many young people spend their holidays hiking—walking long distances from place to place with packs on their backs. It doesn't cost much and is the best way of escaping from crowds. Britain is one of the most thickly populated countries in Europe. Yet there are large areas where there are no towns, only a few old villages and farms.

The Pennine Way goes through a village – an opportunity for a rest

In some of the loneliest and loveliest areas there are long-distance footpaths. The longest, the Pennine Way, is over 300 km long. It winds through forests, along the top of tall, grassy hills, down into deep valleys called 'dales'. Some farms will offer hikers bed and breakfast. There are also Youth Hostels and plenty of places to camp. The Pennine hills are called the backbone of England. Walking in the mountains of Britain can be dangerous. Paths made by sheep suddenly drop into thin air, and every year walkers and rock-climbers fall to their death. Ben Nevis, in Scotland, Britain's highest mountain, is only 1342 m high, but it has a rock face of 300 m from top to bottom.

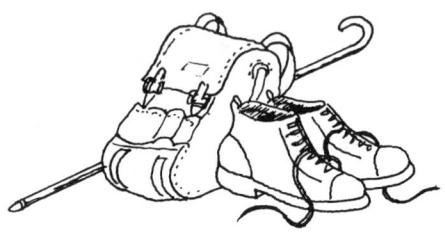

Sports

Football, invented by the British, is the UK's most popular game, even with people who know nothing much about it. Mrs Hastings, for example, married to a bus driver, watches TV every Saturday evening and writes down all the football scores: Tottenham Hotspurs 2 — Manchester United 3; Chelsea 0 — Liverpool 5; West Ham 3 — Newcastle 3. 'Ah, a draw! That's better!' Usually she soon turns the TV off. She is only interested in matches which are drawn. But tonight she is excited. There are nine drawn matches, and they are exactly the same as her own choice which she has sent to the Football Pools for a bet of 50p. She wins £500,000 and gets her name in the national newspapers.

Doing the Football Pools is a mild kind of betting and is very popular. So is having a bet on a horse at the races. Top jockeys become both rich and famous.

Football (soccer) is the national sport and British club teams are often successful in Europe. But British football today has a bad name at home and abroad, because of the violence of some groups of supporters who get drunk and fight rivals. Liverpool supporters caused the deaths of over 30 Italian supporters at a match in Brussels in 1985. Most British supporters dislike violence as much as anybody else, and they are helping the police to put an end to it.

Rugby football is of two kinds. Rugby Union is amateur, which means that players cannot accept payment of any kind.

If they do they may be forbidden to play ever again. Rugby League is professional. It is played mostly in the north of England. The rules of the two games are different, but both are tough and hard. Rugby Union has spread to other countries. The following play it at top level: New Zealand, South Africa, Australia, France, the Argentine, Rumania, Fiji. The USSR, Italy, Japan and Tonga also play.

Cricket is an English game. Not many Scots, Irish or Welsh play it. It is a complicated and mysterious game and is loved by many people, but others are bored by it. Some games go on for five days. It is played by many countries which were once part of the British Empire, but nowhere else. There are amateur cricket clubs all over England, but there is a big difference between the amateur and the professional cricketer. The professional cricketer is in a much higher class. He has to learn many kinds of skills. He has to be an athlete, to run fast and jump and turn like a gymnast. He must be patient, and must not let himself be tricked. Above all, he has to have great courage. This is what a professional cricketer said after being hit on the head by a ball—it took him eight months to recover: 'Cricket is hard, it hurts. It takes a special sort of person to be good at it. But we don't want the danger to be taken out of the game.'

A   Vocabulary

Where are horses kept?   What does a *jockey* do?
What is a *pony*?   What is an *amateur*?
What is the opposite of *false*?   What is a *professional*?
Where do you find *beaches*?   What is a *draw* in football?
Explain *thickly populated*.   Do you enjoy *boring* games?

B   Questions

1 Do the British always stay at home when it rains?
2 What would be the danger if you didn't look where you
   were going when walking on a British mountain?
3 Where could you spend the night when hiking on the
   Pennine Way?
4 Why does Mrs Hastings do the football pools?
5 Name one reason why some football supporters are
   violent.   .
6 Why does a cricketer have to have courage?

C   Grammar

What are the nouns of the following verbs? Here are a few
possible endings. Some verbs are exactly the same as the
noun.

-y   -er   -ing   -ment   -ion   -ery

to enjoy — escape — offer — invent — cause — climb — help
— recover — excite — love — trick

D   Function

Persuasion

Jack wants to take you to a cricket match, but you are not at all keen. Jack tries to persuade you. What does he say?

The weather'll be perfect. — It'll be great fun. — Why not? You'll enjoy it. — They're very comfortable. Really! — It'll be very exciting. — You can always sleep.

You   No, I'd rather not, Jack.
Jack   . . .
You   Because it sounds boring. You told me the game lasts five days.
Jack   No, this is a one-day match . . .
You   One day is still too long.
Jack   . . .
You   It's fine now, but it may not be fine tomorrow. What are the seats like?
Jack   . . .
You   Comfortable! I remember what you said about them— hard wooden benches!
Jack   . . .
You   Sleep! I don't want to spend six hours sleeping on a hard wooden bench!

5   British English – and the languages of the UK

It isn't always easy these days to distinguish between people from different parts of Britain. That's because British people move about the country more than they used to. Northerners come and live in the south. Southerners and East Anglians go to the north, and lots of Scots, Welsh and Irish come and live in England. More people settle in London and the south than in any other region. That is why many Southerners do not really have a special accent—except the Cockneys from the East End of London.

Still, many Northerners think that Southerners have their own accent. They sometimes make fun of the 'southern accent': 'I say, thanks orfully, old chap! It's vair nice of you...'[1] Very few people speak like that today. In fact, it is a form of upper class dialect.

The North still has a character of its own, and Southerners who settle in the North usually take on the Northern way of life. Their children soon pick up the accent from their school friends. The first thing visitors notice is the way Northerners pronounce 'mother', 'much', 'southern', 'done'. In the North these words are pronounced like the standard English 'pull'. Northerners pronounce 'dance', 'chance', 'France' like the 'a' in 'man' – as the Americans do, but when they say 'can't' they pronounce it in the Southern English way, like the 'a' in 'far'. Sometimes Northerners leave out the article, 'the', and also the possessive adjectives, 'my', 'your', 'their', etc.

Here's a Yorkshireman talking to his son, who has just returned from a long stay in London: 'Take feet off t'table, lad. London folk may put feet on t'table, but here we put 'em on t'floor.'[2]

Cockney has a pronunciation, accent and vocabulary unlike any other dialect. Cockneys pronounce 'wait', 'late', 'tray', etc. like 'white', 'light', 'try', etc. 'Wait for me, Dave!' becomes, 'Wite for me, Dive!', and they drop their aitches: 'have' becomes ''ave', etc.

This is how a Cockney tells his friend, Herbert, what happened to Dave when he came home drunk from the pub:

'Poor old Dive! 'e always 'its 'is old woman when 'e's drunk. But this time, when 'e gets 'ome from the pub, 'is old woman 'as 'er bike 'elmet on. But 'e don't see the 'elmet, so 'e 'its it 'stead of 'er 'ead. 'urts 'isself, 'e does!'[3] Cockneys usually tell a story in the present tense.

Many linguists today say that dialects are a natural way of speaking, and that it does not matter if the grammar and pronunciation are not standard English.

Here's some more Cockney: 'I ain't pleased with them repairs wot 'e done.'[4]

Norfolk dialect: 'She say it's wrong. She don't know a lot, do she?'[5]

West Country (Devon and Somerset): 'I be vat and wold, zurr. I stays at wom.'[6]

None of these examples are correct Standard English, but they are quite correct in the regions where they are spoken.

There are several non-English languages spoken in Britain today. Indian immigrants are mostly Hindu and speak Hindi. The Muslim Pakistanis speak Urdu, which is very like Hindi. Their children are bilingual. There are Indian and Pakistani children who speak with perfect Cockney or Northern

English and Welsh signs

accents. English is the language of West Indians, but the dialects of some of the islands are very difficult to understand. West Indian children in Britain, however, often have dialects or accents which are completely British.

There are Welsh people who are doing all they can to preserve the Welsh language. Many Welsh school children have to learn Welsh when they would prefer to learn German or Spanish. Most public signs in Wales are in Welsh as well as in English, even when this isn't really necessary: *Toilet/Toiletd*. The leading members of Plaid Cymru are Welsh-speaking, but not all Welsh-speaking people want independence, or even a separate parliament. English tourists find Welsh place names like Pwllheli impossible to pronounce.

Gaelic on the Hebridean islands of Scotland will not survive as long as Welsh, because children have to go to secondary school on the mainland, where they speak English. Many school leavers find life on the islands too hard and lonely, and move to the cities.

Many Scots who do not speak Gaelic have a broad, colourful dialect that most non-Scots find difficult to understand:

'What do ye think o' yon bonnie lassie, Angus? Dae ye ken her?'

'Ay, but I dinna like her.'

'Why's that, Angus?'

'Well, mun, she's a Sassenach.'[7]

🇬🇧

1 I say, thanks awfully (very much), old chap! It's very nice of you. . .'
2 Take your feet off the table, lad. London folk may put their feet on the table, but here we put them on the floor.
3 Poor old Dave! He always hits his wife when he's drunk. But this time, when he gets home from the pub, his old woman has her bike helmet on. But he doesn't see the helmet, so he hits it instead of her head. Hurts himself, he does!
4 I'm not pleased with those repairs that he's done.
5 She says it's wrong. She doesn't know a lot, does she?
6 I'm fat and old, sir. I stay at home.
7 'What do you think of that good-looking girl, Angus? Do you know her?
   'No, but I don't like her.'
   'Why,s that, Angus?'
   'Well, man, she's English.'
   (Sassenach = 'Saxon')

A sign in English and Gaelic

A   Vocabulary

Find another word or phrase for the following.

to distinguish	*is likely to*
to settle	*correct*
to take on a Northern way of	*bilingual*
life	*to prefer*
to pick up (language)	*independence*
to preserve	*to survive*

B   Questions

1 Where are most Cockneys born?
2 How do Northerners pronounce (a) *can't* (b) *dance*?
3 Find as many words as you can with the same vowel sound as: *done, much, southern, mother.*
4 What would Dave answer if you asked him if he'd hurt his wife?
5 Why do many children in South Wales not want to learn Welsh?
6 Why won't most Hebridean children go on speaking Gaelic?

C   Translation or summary

1   Either translate into your own language, or write in English a summary of the paragraph beginning: 'Gaelic on the Hebridean islands of Scotland will not. . .'
2   Translate into standard English the Cockney passage beginning 'Poor old Dive . . . 'urts isself, 'e does.'

D   Function

Disagreement

Use these phrases to answer the questions in the Dialogue.

Nonsense! — I don't agree — Why should I? — That's a silly argument! — That's unfair.

Phil	You ought to speak Welsh.
Megan	. . .
Phil	Because you're Welsh.
Megan	. . .
Phil	Every Welsh person should learn Welsh.
Megan	. . . Most people can't speak Welsh.
Phil	Well, they're not true Welshmen, then.
Megan	. . .
Phil	I think all Welsh schools should have all their lessons in Welsh.
Megan	. . .

USA

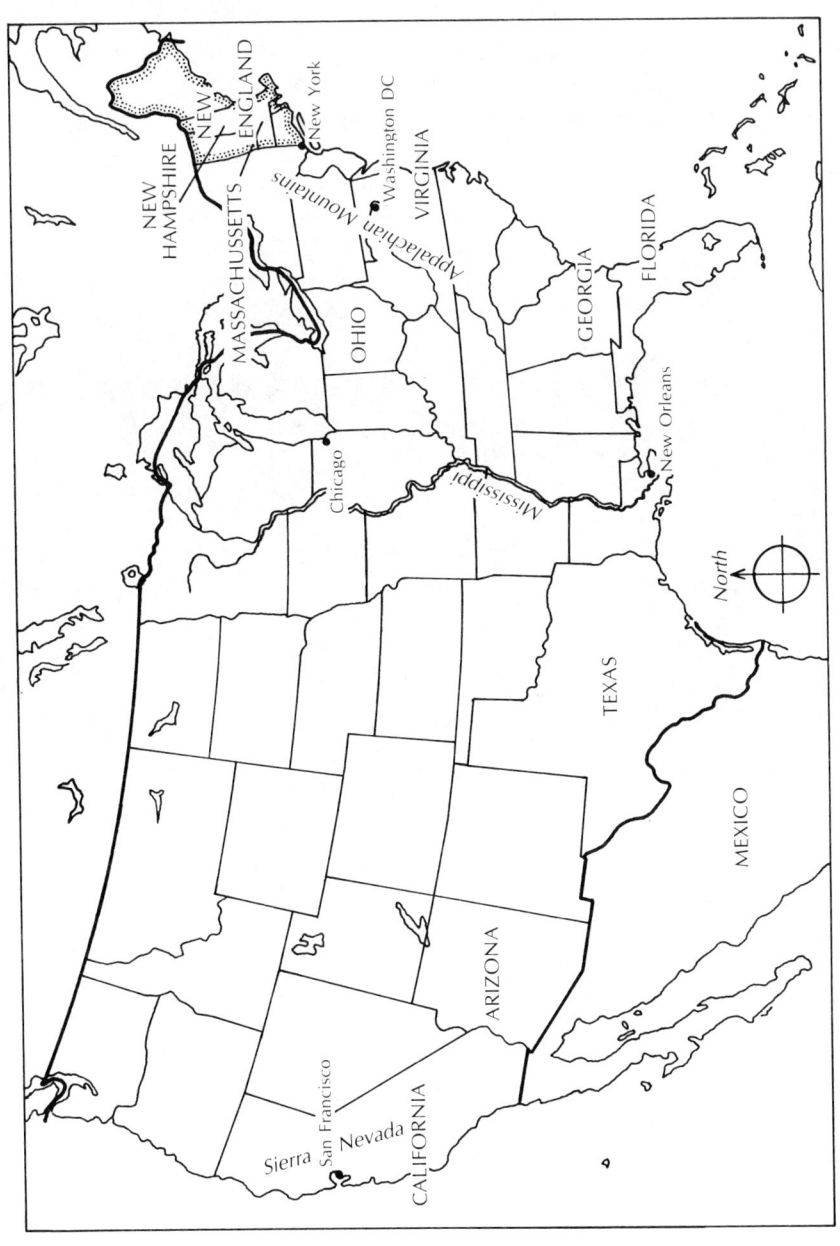

6 How the USA grew

Nowadays people are beginning to use the term 'Native Americans' rather than 'Indians' for the original peoples of America. They probably crossed over from Asia while there was still a land bridge between the two continents.

The first 'white' Americans left England in 1606 to settle in Virginia. They suffered terribly. After five years only 50 colonists were left out of 500. As for the colonists who landed in New England from the *Mayflower* in 1620, more than half died of disease during the first winter.

But the energy and determination which was one day to make the USA a superpower began to show itself. The two colonies were so successful that soon other English men, women and children came out to join them. Virginians who had been farm labourers at home made fortunes out of growing tobacco or cotton on large plantations, and they lived in great houses similar to country houses in England. Colonists no longer judged a man by where he came from, but by what he was. The New Englanders were successful too, especially the Puritans, who believed in a very simple 'pure' form of Protestantism, and who became known as the Pilgrim Fathers. They had left England because the Church would not let them worship as they wished. Their religious faith, their courage and determination gave strength and encouragement to the Americans of the future.

In New England the colonists made friends with the Indians at once, but in Virginia there was no friendship until the chief's daughter, Pocahontas, started visiting the colony

A reconstruction of the Virginian settlement at Jamestown

and fell in love with John Rolfe, a successful tobacco planter. They married, and it is claimed that there are 50,000 descendants from their one son. But the Indians soon realised that the white men were after their land, which they had at first sold to the colonists for almost nothing at all. A deep and bitter hatred grew up between the whites and the Indians.

In 1664, the first African slaves were brought to Virginia and put to work on the tobacco and cotton plantations.

Immigrants continued to come to America, mostly from Britain and Ireland, and by the middle of the 18th century there were thirteen colonies, stretching from New Hampshire and Massachusetts in the north to Georgia in the South. But Britain's old enemy, France, had colonies in Canada and forts down the Ohio and Mississippi rivers. In 1764 the French went to war with the Americans and the British, who fought side by side against them. The American, George Washington, got his first experience of warfare as an officer in a British regiment. The French were heavily defeated and were driven out of North America.

PRESIDENT STREET~
laid out in 1733 as
KING STREET
Renamed after the Revolution

The American Revolutionary War of 1775–83 seemed at the time a stupid and unnecessary war. It was caused by an unpopular British government encouraged by a king, George III, who was a German and knew very little about the colonies. The Government tried to force the colonists to pay taxes which were unjust. The colonists refused to pay them, so the Government sent out more troops. The colonists began to fear that the British Government was threatening their self-governing parliaments. There were powerful members of the British parliament who disagreed strongly with the Government and did their best to prevent a war, and there were many British and American people who felt that a war would be like brother fighting brother, but in 1775 war broke out.

The British army was commanded by a lazy, luxury-loving general who took his mistress around with him in his carriage. The colonists were led by George Washington and helped by friendly Indians. It was an unpleasant war. The British soldiers were not trained to fight guerilla bands or Indians, who attacked them by surprise in the forests. Then the French sent an army to help the Americans, and before long the Americans won their independence.

The thirteen colonies formed a federation, which they called the United States of America. During the next eighty years British, Irish and German immigrants continued to cross the Atlantic to settle in America. The first American pioneers travelled out into the unexplored plains and on across the Rocky Mountains to the burning, waterless deserts of Nevada. To get to San Francisco they crossed the most fearful mountain range of all, the Sierra Nevada. The discovery of gold near San Francisco started a rush to the West, but the rich, fertile earth was the real 'gold' of California. Mountain streams brought water to crops and to plantations of fruit trees. In the foothills of the Rockies cattle ranches were set up and farmers grew corn and wheat in the Great Plains of Montana and North and South Dakota.

After the Civil War (1861–65), which freed the slaves in the South and prevented the Southern states from leaving the Union, the USA really began to grow. Immigrants from all over Europe poured into New York, and from there moved to the factories of the rapidly growing industries, which needed workers. The great transcontinental railway was built, despite fierce attacks by the Indians. In 1860 the population of the USA was about 30,000,000, largely of British origin, but including 3,500,000 African slaves. Today it has swollen to 230,000,000 less than 45% of which are of British origin.

A   Vocabulary

1   What is a *disease*?
2   Make up a sentence using *energy* and *determination*.
3   What is a *plantation*?
4   Name one person that you are a *descendant* of.
5   What is a *slave*?
6   Find another word for *troops*.
7   What is the opposite of: a) *to discourage*   b) *weakness* c) *to win a battle*   d) *hard-working*?

B   Questions

1   What crops did the Virginians grow?
2   What was the religion of the Puritans?
3   Where did Pocahontas meet John Rolfe?
4   How did George Washington get his experience of war?
5   What threat were the American colonists afraid of?
6   In the War of Independence the colonists were helped by two peoples. Who were they?
7   What did the Americans have to cross to reach California in the mid-19th century?

C   Interpreting

Take the paragraph beginning: 'The American Revolutionary War. . .'
Either   1   Translate it into your own language
Or   2   Give a summary of the important facts
               a) in your own language
               or
               b) in English

D   Function

Objections:

'Can I take the car out, Dad?' 'No, son, you can't.'

Make up a dialogue between father and son, using the following notes:

Son   Why not take car?
Dad   Not enough experience; only 17 OR Not good enough driver yet.
Son   Won't damage it; only five miles.
Dad   Freeways crowded now.
Son   Driven in traffic.
Dad   Ice on roads.
Son   Driven when snowing.
Dad   Ice, snow different. Haven't driven icy roads.

7   The American people

The Federal Government

> PRESIDENT Head of State
> SECRETARIES OF STATE appointed by President, form Cabinet
> CONGRESS (Parliament) makes laws; consists of **Senate** and **House of Representatives**. President and Congress are elected by a democratic vote.
> SUPREME COURT consists of nine judges, deals with complaints against the American Constitution, is the American people's greatest safeguard against injustice.

There is no such thing as a typical American, but here are some views of Americans which many think are fair.

Ordinary Americans are friendly and not afraid to show their feelings. They are generous, lively and amusing. They are not as snobbish or class-conscious as the English, and the way people speak is not important to them. A university

These Irish, Poles and Asians come from Hawaii

professor can talk to his students in a broad Brooklyn or Southern accent and no one will be surprised or shocked. In Britain, 'accent snobbery' is dying, but people are sometimes criticised for the way they speak, and this upsets them. However, there is 'money snobbery' in the USA, which sometimes takes strange forms.

The American's dream is success in his job, success earned by his own skill and hard work. There is no one an American admires more that the self-made man, no matter what kind of family he comes from, whereas upper-class people in Britain still tend to dislike self-made men and find them socially unacceptable.

Despite the great wealth of the USA, there is an 'underclass' of some 20 million people, black, white and Hispanic. Because of the awful conditions under which many of these unfortunates live, all hope drains from them and they do not have the strength they need to rise out of their misery. A great part of the violence in American society begins in the ghettos and inner cities where this underclass lives.

The USA is not a welfare state, yet it spends more on the very poor than many nations with a complete welfare system. Even the poorest Americans do not starve to death, and they are not left to die on the street after an accident. Whatever hospital they are taken to, they receive very careful treatment without cost. Even the millions of illegal immigrants who pour every night across the Mexican border get enough food to live on, despite the fact that they are not American citizens. Many Americans feel that the poor and the unemployed get too much welfare. Unemployment pay is certainly much higher than in Britain.

Many foreigners have the false idea that there is no public transport in the USA. Since the vast majority of Americans own at least one car, buses aren't necessary, it is believed, so the very poor have to walk. This is quite untrue. There *is* public transport. There is a cheap and regular bus service in every city. Many cities also have a new subway system, equally cheap. But better-off Americans in many parts of the USA never go by bus. In fact, they wouldn't want to be seen in one, in case someone thought they couldn't afford a car!

The elderly middle class sometimes find themselves in terrible situations. Take Mrs Vorst, a middle-aged widow with a small pension. Her doctor told her she must have an operation immediately. She had the operation, but did not leave the hospital until six weeks later. When she received her bill, she almost fainted, for she wasn't old or poor enough for Medicare (free medical treatment). Then a lawyer heard about her difficulties and suggested she should sue the doctor and the hospital for keeping her in bed too long. The lawyer won her case for her, but he kept as his fee 50% of the money the judge allowed her, so she still couldn't pay the whole bill. Honourable American lawyers are worried by such dishonest members of their profession.

The USA has many serious problems—crime, violence, unlawful immigration across the Mexican border, pollution, unemployment, race relations, and many more. But the Americans face their problems boldly and with determination. Twenty years ago blacks and whites were fighting each other in many American cities. Today more and more blacks hold positions of authority in every walk of life. Fear, dislike, even hatred, are still there in places, but there has been an improvement in race relations that few non-Americans know much about.

There is no Communist party in the USA. It is forbidden, and this pleases most Americans, because they are afraid of

Communism. Some Americans call all socialists and left-wing people in their own and other countries 'Commies'. The Americans believe in 'free enterprise' (the freedom to do business without any interference from the Government). The only political parties which count in the USA are the Democrats and the Republicans. Most Democrats are more liberal than Republicans. They want arms control, more Health Insurance. But there is more difference between the British Labour and Conservative parties than there is between Democrats and Republicans.

A   Vocabulary

1   What would you expect an American to do to show he was *lively*?
2   How would you describe *snobbery*?
3   If you lived *in misery*, how would you feel?
4   What is an *illegal immigrant*?
5   Name some different kinds of *public transport*.
6   When does a person get a *pension*, and what is a *pension*?
7   When you *sue* somebody, what do you expect to get, if you win?
8   What happens when there is an *improvement* in race relations?
9   What is *Commies* short for?

B   Questions

1   Why do Americans admire self-made men?
2   In cities where there are many poor people, where do most of them live?
3   Why are things not so bad for poor Americans as some people think?
4   Why are many Americans not happy about their welfare system?
5   Why don't some Americans like to be seen in a bus?

6   What did Mrs Vorst think about the hospital bill?
7   Why couldn't Mrs Vorst pay the whole hospital bill after the lawyer had won her case?
8   What is free enterprise? In what way is Communism different?

C   Grammar

Imagine that paragraph 4 (Despite the great wealth of the USA . . .) is part of a talk given by a Mr Pepper. You are a newspaper reporter. Rewrite the paragraph (and the one that follows, if you have time) in *reported speech*.

eg 'Mr Pepper claimed/said/told us that in spite of the great wealth . . . there *was* . . .

You will have to add several times 'he said', or 'he told us'.

D   Function

Doubt and certainty

I'm sure they do./I'm not sure. — I don't know. — Yes, it (he) is./No, it (he) isn't. — I doubt it. — I think so./I don't think so. — Of course there are./there aren't.

Answer the following questions with one of the phrases above:

1   Is the average American taller than the average Englishman?
2   Is the Empire State Building in New York?
3   Are there any black policemen in the New York Police?
4   How much does the President of the USA earn a year?
5   Is the Mississippi a lake?
6   Are there any polar bears in the Californian desert?
7   Are you sure the Americans speak English?

8 Working and getting to work in an industrial superpower

The United States has most of what every country would like to have—coal and oil and other minerals, cereals (wheat, barley, maize), beef cattle, fruit plantations of all kinds, as well as flourishing industries. Yet, as in most countries, there is unemployment and the fear of unemployment, and few people like being unemployed more than the Americans. They are paid well, even in quite simple jobs, and their taxes are low, so they don't often come out on strike for unimportant reasons. Union officials in the factories are employed not only to make sure the workers get fair treatment, but also to see that they work as well as they can.

Managers and workers usually get on well together. They call each other by their first names, and the bosses usually give more encouragement than criticism. They also let the Union leaders know how much money the firm has in the bank, so that Unions do not usually ask for higher wages when the firm can't afford it. They know it doesn't help them if they get a firm into difficulties. A lot of Americans do two jobs at the same time, and unemployment is not as high as in many countries. People are not popular if they refuse to take a job that is offered to them and live instead on unemployment pay.

During most of the 19th century, Britain was the world's greatest industrial power. Then, towards the end of the century, the Americans began to catch up. By 1913, Henry Ford was mass-producing his Model T Ford, using machines to make the parts. The USA now makes each year more cars, trucks and buses than are made in the whole of Europe. Today 85% of American families own at least one car, and 35% own two or more. There are more than 3,000,000 miles (4,830,000 km) of paved roads in the USA.

Gene, an American, explained to Andy, a visiting Englishman, how important the automobile is. 'Our whole social system and our whole industrial system are built round the automobile. We cannot do without it.'

'Isn't that true of all modern societies?' Andy asked.

'Yeah,[1] but more so in the US. Most British commuters drive, or are driven, to the station, and from there travel by

train to London. From the railway terminal[2] they go on to their place of work by underground, bus or cab[3].'

'You, too, have commuters that come in to Grand Central or Penn stations,' Andy replied. 'I've seen them. And from there they take a taxi or the Subway.'

'Yeah,' said Gene, 'but most people in the USA drive to work. American cities have at least one freeway (motorway with at least six lanes), often coming right into the city. So commuting by automobile is no longer the headache it was. It means that people can get right away from work and live in the suburbs. Many businesses have moved out of the inner cities, too. It's fine for the bosses and office workers. They avoid the hassle* of the big city. But it's not so good for the blacks who still live in the inner cities. Most of them just lose their jobs.'

'So your railways don't have much to do now?' Andy asked.

'Oh, yes, they do! A train can be made up of over 100 freight cars[4], loaded with coal, iron ore, wheat and petroleum and pulled by three huge locomotives[5] – it's a great sight! But trucks[6] carry the most valuable freight, like manufactured goods or food.'

'What about passengers?'

'They travel by plane, except for very short distances. Most towns, even quite small ones, have a comfortable airport. All airlines are independent, but airlines get extra money from the Government so they can keep the cost of fares down.'

'Don't Americans use their cars for business trips?'

'Not for long journeys. The distance between cities is usually too great. From New York to New Orleans, for example, is 2883 km. If air passengers need a car the other end, they rent one. There are car rental firms in every airport.'

'Do you build most of your own planes?'

'Sure, we do! We build more planes than any other country in the world. Your BA (British Airways), and most European airlines, in fact, fly American aircraft, especially Boeings—and as for our space programme, we're miles ahead of everyone.'

Andy laughed. 'What about the Russians?'

The businessmen who create so much of the USA's wealth often work extremely hard. Some of them drink too many cocktails, smoke too much, and sooner or later start to worry about their health. Their doctors tell them, if they carry on like that they'll get heart trouble, they must lose weight and pay more attention to what they eat. So, since jogging is now considered to be dangerous for some people, they take up a health diet (eat special food).

hassle tiring noise and movement

1 Yes
2 terminus
3 taxi
4 carriages
5 engines
6 lorries

The Pentagon, the headquarters of the US Defense Department in Washington DC, has 17 miles of corridors and 44,000 telephones.

A Mississippi oil platform

A   Vocabulary

Which of these words would you use to fill the gaps in the passage below?

strike — fair treatment — to get on — criticism — afford — commuter — inner city — fares — trip — cocktail — train — office

I don't ... with my Dad. He could easily ... to buy me a car, but he says I'm not a ... because we live in the ... only five minutes walk from the .... When I want to see my girlfriend, I have to make the ... by .... I'd go by air, but the ... are too high. My Dad's workers have just gone on .... They say he's not giving them .... I think their ... is completely fair. We're having a ... party this evening. Why don't you come?

B   Questions

1 What do American workers fear more than most people?
2 How does it help a firm, if the Union knows how much money that firm has in the bank?
3 In what ways are American and British commuters different?
4 Why is commuting by car much easier in the USA than it was?
5 What has happened to many of the blacks who live in the inner cities?
6 What are freight trains used for?
7 What advice would you give to some American businessmen?

C   Grammar

What will happen when the new freeway is built? Take the paragraph beginning: 'Yes, but most people in the USA ...' and turn it into the *future*. Replace the first two sentences with 'When our new freeway is built, commuting by automobile... etc.'

D   Function

Warning someone

I warn you — I advise you to/not to — It will be dangerous for you if — You know what will happen if — You should be careful to/not to ...

Fill in the gaps for the Doctor, using one of the warning phrases above.

Doctor   I warn you that you are working too hard. You will be seriously ill if you go on like this.
Mr Gold   I only work 10 hours a day, and I sometimes bring work home.

Doctor   ...
Mr Gold   I only smoke 30 cigarettes a day. I'd hate to smoke less.
Doctor   ...
Mr Gold   But I love butter and cream, and I enjoy a good meal.
Doctor   ...
Mr Gold   How can I lose weight? I'm sure I don't weigh too much.
Doctor   ...
Mr Gold   But there's no time to take exercise.
Doctor   ...
Mr Gold   OK, Doctor, if you say so. I'll go on a diet, give up smoking and take more exercise. I don't want to have a heart attack!

9   Americans at play

Wayne and Cheryl Lord walked carefully down the steep track from the Appalachian Trail, which they had been following for the last six days. The Trail runs for 3000 km through thick forest along the top of the Appalachian Mountains. Every 12 or 13 km there are camp sites and rough shelters. Wayne and Cheryl had so far spent every night in one of these shelters, but now Cheryl was determined to leave the Trail and find a motel. 'I want to take a bath,' she said. Wayne secretly wanted to spend every night outdoors, so that he could tell his friends about it, but he never argued with his wife. He was one of those American husbands who work really hard to buy their wives every possible machine that will save work in the kitchen. Cheryl was grateful for his efforts, but she didn't often tell him so.

Often after supper they went to the movies together, or sat and watched TV, and once a week they went to the neighbourhood Community Centre with their teenage son and daughter, where they swam or played basketball. But most evenings Wayne went to the golf club. Or he went to his club, Bearskins, where women were not allowed and where he and his buddies[1] discussed everything from the President of the United States to the baseball game between the Detroit Tigers and the Chicago White Sox. His sixteen year old daughter, Chrissie, wanted to know more about the Bearskin Club. 'You never tell us anything about it, Dad. What secrets are you hiding from us?'

'It's no good, Chrissie,' her mother said. 'He'll never tell you. He won't even tell me. I don't think anything happens there.'

'Where are you off to tonight, Chrissie?' her father asked.

'To wait table[2] at the Steak House with Tommy. Then we'll probably go for a drive in his new car. Don't look so anxious, Dad, he's a good driver.' She turned to her mother, 'What are you going to read at the Poetry Reading Club, Mom?'

'Robert Frost,' said Cheryl.

One weekend the Lords gave a cocktail party. As the weather was fine, they stood around the swimming pool. There was an English woman present who asked for a martini. She was surprised to find that it tasted more like gin than martini. As she didn't like gin, she asked if she could have a martini without the gin. It wasn't possible. In the USA bottles of martini are usually sold already mixed with gin.

The guests could hear the sound of jazz coming from upstairs. The Lords' son, Jason, has a large collection of jazz discs[3]. He is a great admirer of the black trumpeter, Louis Armstrong.

American Sport

'Why are you Americans so good at sport, Gene?' Andy asked. 'Is it because you're so keen to win?'

'Perhaps. Our attitude to sports is different from yours. We're more professional about it. We don't waste our time and energies training without coaching. We have first-class

coaches who know exactly how to get the best out of us. Top stars have computers to help them—what's the best speed for the first 200 metres; at what point they should start the final sprint, and so on.'

'Hasn't your climate something to do with it? You can train out of doors the whole year. I'd say that training in the rain and grey skies of northern Europe would upset any athlete! Then there's the question of money.'

'Yes. If a promising athlete is discovered, somebody somewhere will provide the money for the very best training, however poor he or she is. Many of our black athletes are among the very best. Think how many Olympic medals they win! They're also first-class at football, baseball and basketball. They wouldn't succeed as they do if they weren't given sports scholarships to college. It isn't supposed to be done, but it is, and good luck to 'em. Sports still give blacks a better chance of success than most things.'

'The attitude to the Olympics has changed—the "enjoy yourself" amateur approach has gone.'

'But athletes are breaking records all the time. You can't have it both ways. Winning has become a part of national pride, and many of the winners become world-famous—and rich! Quite a few of your British athletes come over here to train, you know. But we don't overdo it, as the Russians and East Germans seem to do. Their athletes have such a strict routine, I guess they don't have time to enjoy themselves at all. Still, look at their list of winners and broken records! Since 1965, Russia has come first four times, and the USA three times, but the crazy thing is, the USA and Russia have each won a total of 260 gold medals.'

'And what about Britain?'

'The Brits[4] have won 24 golds during the same period, and – listen to this – Australia has won twice as many as Britain.'

Flag-waving majorettes

'Tell me, at college football matches does each team have to have an army of girls, all dressed the same? They march up and down to military music and have a sort of leader at the front, waving a stick.'

'The girl with the stick is the cheer leader. It takes a long time to learn how to handle that stick. Why do we have them? Their cheers help us.'

1 friends
2 wait at table
3 records
4 British

A   Vocabulary

1 Explain the meaning of *camp site*.
2 What are a) a *trail* b) a *buddy* c) a *trumpet*?
3 If you're *sprinting*, how are you running?
4 What does a *coach* do?
5 How do you feel if you're *enjoying* yourself?
6 What is the meaning of *breaking the 1000 m record*?
7 With what part of the body do you *cheer*?

B   Questions

1   Why does Cheryl want to leave the trail, and why does Wayne not want to?
2   What do the Lords do together once a week?
3   How does Wayne spend most of his evenings?
4   What is Cheryl going to do at the Poetry Reading Club?
5   Why couldn't the English woman drink her martini?
6   What helps some black athletes to succeed?
7   What does Gene think about the Russian way of training?

C   Grammar

Fill in the gaps with the right preposition.

1   I'm grateful . . . your help.
2   He drank some orange juice mixed . . . gin.
3   She's very good . . . tennis.
4   A week in the sun would be best . . . him.
5   I asked him . . . his help.
6   We argued . . . it.
7   He's training . . . the race.
8   He hasn't a chance . . . winning.
9   He's standing . . . the front.

D   Function

Regret and sympathy after an accident

I'm awfully sorry about it. — It must have been a terrible shock for you. — Are you all right now? — What bad luck! — Here, take my hand! — I can understand how angry you feel.

Girl/Boy   I was knocked off my bike by a car.
You   . . .
Girl/Boy   Yes, I'm all right now, but I never saw the car coming.

You   . . .
Girl/Boy Yes, it was. And it didn't stop.
You   . . .
Girl/Boy I was going to spend the day at the sea with my
            girl/boyfriend.
You   . . . You can spend the day with me, if you like.

10   How the Americans talk English

> Until the 1860s, most of the immigrants to the USA
> were British, Irish or German. Since World War 2,
> nearly a million Britons have settled in the USA, far
> more than from any other European country.

Although the USA is by far the most powerful of the English-speaking countries, the English that is taught in most parts of the world is British English. Besides, British English is the 'mother' language upon which all English, written or spoken, is based, including American English. In fact, most Americans like the way the English speak, and there are New England families whose accent is closer to standard British English than is the accent of the educated Scot. Many Americans, including some who have no British blood in them, regard Britain culturally as the Mother Country. Americans read English literature without any difficulty at all, and British readers of early 20th century American literature have no problems either. But for the last fifty years the Americans have been inventing a whole bunch of new words and phrases, many of which have already reached the UK and the whole English-speaking world.

However, there are occasional misunderstandings.

Smart Englishwoman to smart American woman on a Californian beach It's the first time I've bathed for years.

American (amazed) Is that so? I can't believe it!

Englishwoman It's true. You see, the water at home's always so cold.
American But ... but surely you have hot water in England?
Englishwoman (laughs) Of course, but not in the sea!

In American English, 'to bathe' means 'to wash, have a bath'. In British English, it means 'to go swimming'.

There can be similar misunderstandings over the word 'pants', though most English people know that Americans call trousers 'pants'.

American girl I never wear pants. They don't suit me.
English girl Really? Couldn't that be a bit embarrassing?
American girl Embarrassing? Why?
English girl Well – that short skirt you're wearing ...
American girl Oh, my! But I wear panties!

In British English, 'pants' are undergarments. However, young people in Britain do sometimes say 'pants' for 'trousers'.

Serious English authors, without knowing it, use many phrases of American origin, eg a *way of life*; *teenager*; *boyfriend* and *girlfriend*; *baby-sitter*; *TV*; 'after ten years he visited his *home town*'; 'he is a *commuter*, going up to his London office every day'; 'he *beat up* the prisoner'.

Spanish and German street signs

'Ah can't unnerstan' a word yer sane.[1] There are dialects in the USA which are as difficult to understand as those in the UK, and they go back to the days when the American states were separate colonies. The Southerners of Virginia, Georgia, the two Carolinas and the other Southern colonies were cut off from the North by broad rivers, mountains and thick forests. Left to themselves they developed a way of speaking that is so difficult to imitate that some American actors and actresses refuse to take Southern parts. Vowels and consonants have their own special sounds, and the Southern vocabulary and grammar is often different from standard American English. Southerners tend to speak slowly and their speech is often known as the 'Southern drawl'.

In the following passage words are spelt phonetically:

'Hev off yore coat and hate. Thar's a cheer by the far. Set down. Ho minny miles hev ye-uns walked?[2]

Many foreign languages are spoken in the USA, but by far the most important is Spanish. Nobody knows exactly how many Mexicans have crossed the border without permits since World War 2. But there are about 4,500,000 Mexicans in California, 3,000,000 in Texas, 1,000,000 in Arizona and New Mexico. There are 1,000,000 Cubans in Florida (Miami is about 50% Hispanic), 1,500,000 Puerto Ricans in New York and 600,000 in Chicago. About 5% of the American population speak Spanish as their first language, and a great many of these cannot speak more than a word or two of English.

1 I can't understand a word you're saying!
2 Take off your coat and hat. There's a chair by the fire. Sit down. How many miles have you walked?

'Over one quarter of the more than four million state school students in California now come from homes where a language other than English is frequently spoken.'

Fred Tempes, in *EFL Gazette*, November 1985

A   Vocabulary

1   What is the meaning of 'he has no *British blood* in him'?
2   What other words could you use instead of *bunch*? (p. 58, 7th line up)
3   What do you mean when you say 'it was a *misunderstanding*'
4   When might you be *embarrassed*? Give an example.
5   Why do people with young families sometimes have *baby-sitters*?
6   What other words could you use instead of *beat up*? (p. 59, last line of passage)

B   Questions

1   Explain the meaning of the phrase: 'Britain is culturally the Mother Country of the USA'.
2   Show that you understand the difference between the American meaning and the British meaning of the verb 'to bathe'.
3   Where do most of the Spanish-speaking Americans come from?

C   Rewriting

Turn the dialogue 'Smart Englishwoman to smart American woman . . .' into a piece of descriptive writing:

> eg 'Hazel Booker had just come out of the sea on a Californian beach and was sitting beside her American friend, Judy Shuttle . . .'

Do not use any dialogue, but you may add a few details if you like.

D   Function

Understanding: American policeman meets English motorist

I'm afraid I don't understand. — Just repeat what you said, please. — Yes, but please explain what you mean by 'trunk'. — Could you say that again, please? — Oh, is that what you call it?

Use the phrases above to fill in the gaps in the following dialogue.

Policeman	I want to see inside your trunk*.
Englishwoman	...
Policeman	Lady, you heard me! Open your trunk.
Englishwoman	...
Policeman	Cut it out, lady! You understand English.
Englishwoman	...
Policeman	No funny business. Just open your trunk.
Englishwoman	... Are *you* trying to be funny?
Policeman	(goes to back of car). Just give me your trunk key.
Englishwoman	... Oh. In England we call it the 'boot'.

* One meaning for 'trunk' in British English – and also in American English – is 'large case for carrying things when travelling'.

Canada

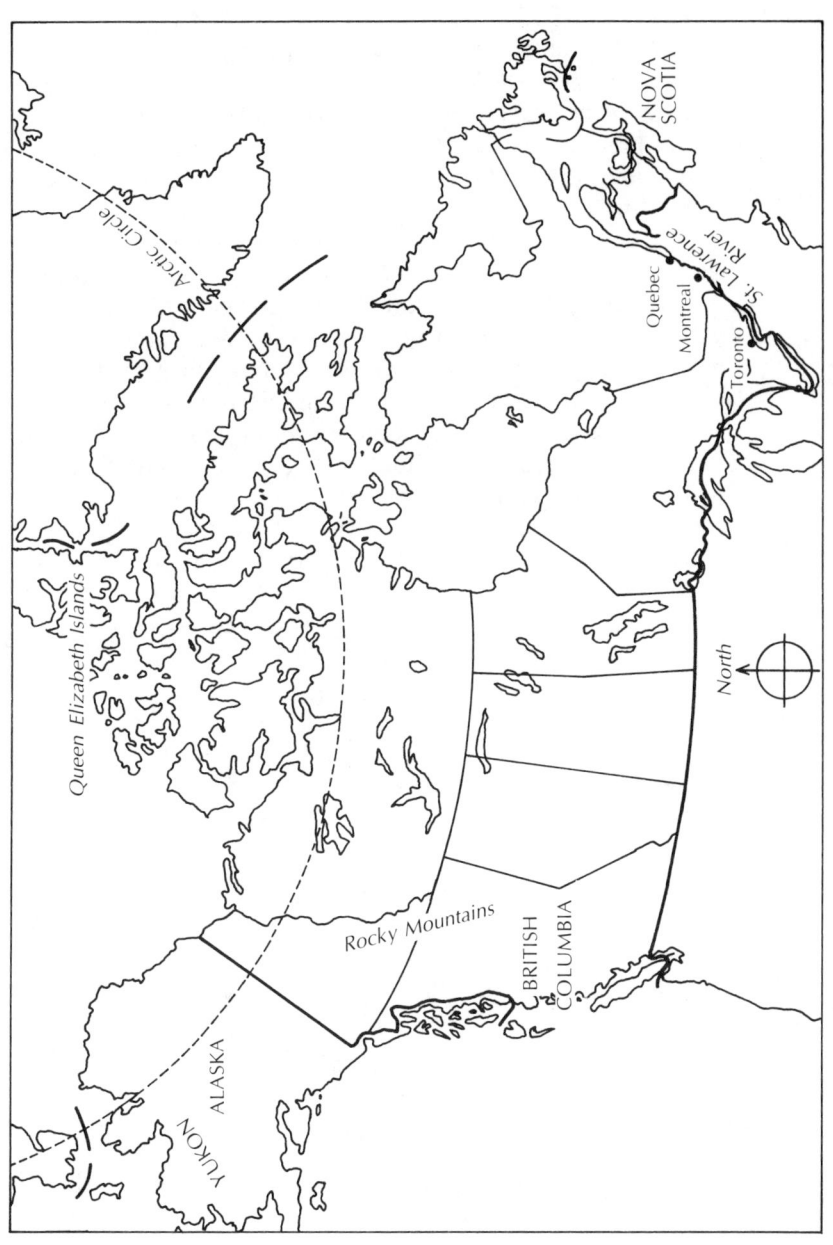

11   The making of Canada

John Cabot, an Italian sea captain in the pay of the British, discovered Canada in 1497, five years after Columbus discovered America. He planted a huge cross on the shore and then sailed home, with the news that he had reached north east China, the land of the Great Khan, and that the sea was full of fish.

In 1534, the French explorer, Jacques Cartier, sailed right down the St Lawrence River until he could go no further. Among the great forests along the shore he met Indians who welcomed him, but in return he kidnapped some of their chiefs. He was the first European to treat the Indians with cruelty and treachery. It was almost another hundred years before French colonists settled on the banks of the St Lawrence and founded Quebec. They were sent there to give food and shelter to the French fur traders, who were carrying on a profitable trade with the Indians.

By the middle of the 18th century, the French in North America realised that they could not avoid a fight to the death with the British and their American colonists, but back in France the French King, Louis XV, was too busy with his

Storming the cliffs at Quebec

wars with Prussia to bother much about what was going on in the 'Land of Ice and Snow'. So the French troops in Canada did not receive the supplies they needed so badly, and the few ships that did try to get through were usually captured by British warships.

Yet this colonial war ended in a famous battle. The British surprised the French by climbing the cliffs at Quebec in the middle of the night. After their defeat, the French were forced to give up every inch of land in North America. But the British allowed the French colonists, all 60,000 of them, to stay on, and they did not try and change the French way of life or their religion. The French were all Catholics. But the British warned them that Louis XV of France was no longer their King. Their King, from now on, would be King George III of England.

At that time there were very few British colonists in Canada. The first British settlers in Canada were American refugees who refused to fight against the British army in the Revolutionary War, because they felt they were more British than American. They called themselves Loyalists, but their fellow Americans accused them of being traitors and took away their possessions. 80,000 Loyalists helped the British to defend Canada against an invading American army during the Revolutionary War.

During the first half of the nineteenth century one million immigrants, mostly British, settled in Canada, but there were hardly any French immigrants from France. However, the French Canadians' birth rate was high, so that in just over two centuries the French Canadian population increased from 60,000 to 6 million.

> 'We have two races, two languages, two systems of religious belief, two sets of laws ... two systems of everything.'
> Canadian journalist

Joe Mulloy, a student from London, was interested in the French Canadians and asked a Quebecois friend, Pierre

Charcot, about them. 'What would happen, Pierre, if Quebec declared itself independent?'

'It'd be very unfortunate for everybody,' Pierre replied. 'It's what a lot of French Canadians want, but I don't think it'll ever happen.'

'Why do they want to leave Canada?' asked Joe.

'Because Quebec is much more French than Canadian. The way of life of Anglophone (English-speaking) Canadians is American, with some British mixed in.'

'French and British Canadians get on all right, don't they?'

'Well, Montreal is a bit of a problem. It's Francophone (French-speaking) and the second biggest city in Canada. But there are a lot of Anglophone businessmen there, and they usually employ Anglophone workers. Now there are more and more Francophone employers who will only employ Francophone workers! So more and more Anglophones are moving to Ontario where mostly English is spoken.'

> 'You ask a Canadian who he is, and he will say "I am not an American".'
> Laurier Lapierre

Canada spread from the Atlantic right across the prairies* and the Rocky Mountains to British Columbia; and northwards to the bare but beautiful Yukon and the ice-covered islands of the Arctic. The pioneer farmers found that the black earth of the prairie provinces could grow some of the finest grain in the world. The tracks of the Canadian Pacific Railway pushed on westwards through Indian lands. To protect their land the Indians made fierce attacks on the railway-builders and the farmers.

Canada moved slowly towards self-rule during the second half of the nineteenth century. A federation of provinces was formed from Nova Scotia on the Atlantic coast to British Columbia on the far side of the Rockies. In 1936 Canada became a Dominion (a self-governing nation) within the British Commonwealth and Empire. The Dominions of Canada, New Zealand and South Africa went to war alongside Britain in 1918 and again in 1939.

*prairies wide, flat grasslands

A   Vocabulary

1   What do you do when you *kidnap* someone?
2   Make up an example of an act of *treachery*.
3   What sort of *supplies* would the French troops in Canada have received?
4   What is a *refugee*?
5   What English verb does *birth rate* suggest?
6   If you are *loyal* you . . . (Finish the sentence).
7   What is an *Anglophone*?
8   Explain what a *federation* is, or give an example.

B   Questions

1   Why did the first French settlers go to Quebec?
2   Where is the 'Land of Ice and Snow'?
3   What did the French lose after their defeat at Quebec?
4   Where did the first British settlers in Canada come from?
5   How did the French Canadians manage to increase their population to 6,000,000 in two centuries?
6   What language, or languages, are spoken in Montreal?
7   What did the pioneer farmers grow on the prairies?
8   What change took place when Canada became a Dominion?

C   Grammar

Comparisons. Complete the following sentences.

Examples   Quebec . . . French . . . Canadian
Quebec *is more* French *than* Canadian.
He . . . (happy) . . . Ann.
He *is happier than* Ann.

1   The St Lawrence . . . (long) . . . the Thames.
2   Louis XIV . . . (interested) in war with Prussia . . . with Canada.

3 The British . . . (good seamen) . . . the French.
4 There . . . British Canadians . . . French Canadians.
5 The Atlantic Ocean . . . (wide) . . . the prairies.
6 New York . . . (big) . . . Montreal.

D   Function

Answering questions

Yes, he/she/it is, they are. — Yes, he/she/it does, they
do. — No, he/she/it isn't, they aren't. — No, he/she/it doesn't,
they don't.

1 Do the French rule Canada?
2 Is the Queen still head of the Canadian Government?
3 Are the British still rulers of Canada?
4 Do French and British Canadians live happily together?
5 Do French businessmen in Montreal speak French together?
6 Are all French Canadians Francophones?

12   People and government of Canada

Canada is a good example of the way peoples of different
ways of life and different languages can live side by side
under one government. The population of Canada has risen
from 11.5 million in 1941 to 25 million in 1980. Most of the
newcomers are from Europe, Asia and the USA, so that today
less than 44% of Canada's population is of British origin.
Quebec Province is still 90% French. There are some groups
of French Canadians in Ontario and Manitoba, but the
numbers are quite small.

There are many Indians, Pakistanis and Chinese, and also
blacks from the USA, among the immigrants who are
pouring into Canada now. Some Canadians are afraid that

before long Canada will have more coloured citizens than white. Other Canadians are disturbed by the growing racism in their country. Canada, like so many other countries, has only just begun to treat her own non-white citizens, the Eskimos (or Inuit) and the Indians, as generously as they deserve. The Indian and Eskimo populations have grown quite a lot in the last few years. The government is at last realising that it has a duty towards these people that it has neglected for so long.

All Canadian children have to learn both French and English at school, but Francophones and Anglophones do not enjoy learning each other's language. Still, most Quebecois middle class families living in Montreal are bilingual—they speak English and French equally well.

Until the Second World War, every Canadian province except Quebec was overwhelmingly British, both by blood and in feeling. Some Canadians were more patriotic than the British themselves and were really angry if anyone walked out of a cinema while *God Save the King* was being played. Now Canadians think of themselves as a people in their own right, not tied to either Britain or the USA. The USA has not been a threat to Canada for almost two hundred years. In fact, the 6,416 km US–Canadian frontier, the longest continuous frontier in the world, has no wire fence, no soldiers, no guns on either side. It is called 'the Border'.

'Living next to the United States is in some ways like sleeping with an elephant.'
Premier Trudeau, Prime Minister

Joe Mulloy met an American girl, Suzie, who had moved to Toronto. 'Why did you leave the USA?' he asked.

'Because I have a boyfriend here, but chiefly because Detroit, where we used to live, is such an awful city. My mother and father were both mugged*.'

'You mean there's no violence in Toronto?'

'Very little' said Suzie. You can walk anywhere, night or day, or ride the Subway[1], and feel quite safe. There are really

*mugged attacked and robbed

no poor neighbourhoods in Toronto, no ghettos. And the laws against guns are stricter.'

'But don't you find Canada dull after America?'

'It was rather dull, people say, just after the war, but it isn't now, not since all the European immigrants have settled here. I've made friends with some Italians. They've opened a restaurant, and it's very good, too. There are thousands of Italians in Toronto now. That's a lot, and they bring the place alive.'

'Still, don't you find Toronto rather provincial?' asked Joe.

'Provincial? You're kidding[2]! It has a population of three million, you know. Canada is an exciting place to be these days, because it's building up a culture of its own. Lots of Canadians are crazy about music and the theatre.'

'So you don't find life very different, then?'

'Well, if you were taken up in a plane and dropped in a Toronto shopping mall,* you wouldn't know if you were in Canada or the USA. But life here is calmer,' said Suzie.

The Canadian government is more British in style than American, except that it is a federal government. The head of government is the Prime Minister, often called the 'PM', as in Britain.

The Federal Government has a Senate and House of Commons, and each province also has a House of Commons.

Canada now belongs to the Commonwealth of Nations (nations which once belonged to the British Empire.) Her ties with the mother country are not as strong as they were. She has a new flag which has two red bands at either end with a red maple leaf in the middle. The maple tree is the national tree of Canada. In the fall[3] maple leaves turn a brilliant red and orange.

Queen Elizabeth II is still Queen of Canada. She is head of the government, as in Britain, but has a Governor-General to represent her. She is still quite popular among Anglophone Canadians, but she is more popular still in the USA!

    1   Underground (railway)   3   autumn
                        2   joking

*mall covered shopping area without traffic

A   Vocabulary

1   What does *pouring* suggest here? (page 68, bottom line)
2   Explain the word *racism*.
3   What do you do if you are *generous*?
4   'Crazy about music and the theatre'. What does *crazy* mean here?
5   Explain *provincial*.
6   What are *ties* with the mother country?
7   Does an *immigrant* come into a country or leave it?

B   Questions

1   What was the increase in Canada's population between 1841 and 1980?
2   What is the meaning of *overwhelmingly* British?
3   What shows that the Canadians do not regard the USA as a threat?
4   Name one difference between Detroit and Toronto.
5   What is the 'PM'?
6   At what time of the year are maple leaves red and orange?

C   Grammar

Fill in the gaps in the following sentences, using the relative pronoun: *what, that, which, who,* or nothing (eg *the man he saw*). If you think two or more of the pronouns will fit, include them.

1   French is the language . . . he speaks best.
2   I know . . . he wants.
3   The girl . . . came to see me was a Canadian.
4   He didn't get the job in Montreal, . . . really upset him.
5   The thing . . . upset him most was being called a racist.
6   I don't know . . . of them did it.
7   I think it was that man . . . we saw on the ice rink.

D   Function

Showing interest

What's it like? — That would be marvellous. — I'd love to. — I've never been out of Europe. — You certainly make me want to go.

Young man	Have you ever been to Canada?
Girl	No ...
Young man	Would you like to see Canada?
Girl	Oh, yes ... , but tell me ... ?
Young man	Well, the most exciting part is the Rocky Mountains. There are snowy peaks, and lakes, and great forests.
Girl	...
Young man	I live in Vancouver. We could go for drives in my car.
Girl	...

13   Life and industry in Canada's far north

Canada buys most of what she needs from the USA, and the USA buys most of what Canada sells. Canada's prairie provinces grow vast crops of grain, but the great forests which stretch from the Pacific to the St Lawrence, and far up into the Northwest Territories, are much more valuable. Canada is one of the world's greatest timber producers.

Canada also has many different minerals. In the Northwest Territories and the Yukon, prospectors* found that many of these minerals lay in the Arctic: lead, zinc, copper, gold, silver, coal, uranium, asbestos, above all oil and natural gas.

Few places are more windswept or bitterly cold than the Canadian Arctic, an empty, treeless, icy land stretching all the way from Alaska to Greenland. From September until

prospectors men who look for minerals

June, everything lies buried beneath snow and ice. Yet in the short summer, rocks and pools gleam in the midnight sun (for a few days in midsummer the sun never sets). Tiny willows burst into leaf, and there are places where millions of wild flowers, of all colours, spread for miles across the ice-cold earth.

This Arctic land is called the tundra. It is the land of the Eskimo, or Inuit, as they prefer to be called. In their own language, 'Inuit' means 'the people', whereas 'Eskimo' is an Indian word meaning 'eaters of raw flesh'. The Inuit used to be nomads, hunting seals on the ice in winter and caribou on the tundra in summer. They slept in tents made of caribou skins. They were a peaceful people who lived their lives cheerfully, and they joked and laughed a great deal. Then the white hunters came and shot caribou and polar bears and musk oxen and wolves, and the government had no control over them. Other white men came in search of minerals beneath the tundra and found oil and natural gas. The arrival of the white men with their guns and machinery changed the lives of the Inuit. They gradually gave up living as nomads and moved into settlements, where they had little to do except drink in the saloons. They were no longer happy and they did not laugh very often.

But now things have changed once more. The Inuit have started hunting again—with guns and snowmobiles. The hunters still live in tents, but they keep a store of canned food in case they cannot get enough to eat from their hunting. The government has built towns for them, like Inuvik, where they can get training in many kinds of jobs, and where their children can go to school. Their health is looked after, and the Inuit now live longer than they did when they were nomads.

Some years ago the oilmen found oil, and also natural gas, beneath the sea not far from the Mackenzie River, and further north still, on the Queen Elizabeth Islands. The search for oil and gas in these frozen regions is a dangerous adventure, almost as dangerous as the gold rush across the Rocky Mountains in the last century. Between the Queen Elizabeth Islands and the North Pole there is no more land, only snow and ice which never melts in summer or winter. The oilmen have only one link with civilisation, the aeroplane, and their lives depend on the skill of the pilots. There have been some bad crashes.

'It's just about as far north as you can go,' Mark Grigson, a roughneck*, said in an interview with a reporter. 'Look at the map and you'll see. You can only get there by plane, and that can be frightening, because we're right near the magnetic pole, which means you can't use a compass. We don't see the sun for most of the year. It makes you miserable after a while, so we work for 12 hours a day for two weeks, then go south for a week's vacation[1] ... It's an awful place. The temperature sometimes stays at 60° below zero for weeks and weeks, and there are blinding snowstorms. The cold is unbelievable. I once saw a man with all the skin torn off his hand. He'd lost one of his gloves and took hold of an iron railing. It was just as if it was red hot .... You can see why alcohol is forbidden up there. You could easily drink too much, and then you'd be done for*. Summer's not much better, though at least we don't get mosquitoes as far north as that. But there are plenty of fogs, and polar bears are a danger, too. I had to shoot one once—in self protection. Still, we're pretty comfortable in our huts .... There's plenty of gas up there. The problem is getting it back to civilisation. But the company reckon they can do it by pipeline—once they've found enough gas to make it worth the cost. The construction of a pipeline will cost a fortune.'

The attitude of these new pioneers is, 'Anything is possible if you really want it.'

1   holiday

A   Vocabulary

1   What produces *timber?*
2   Where are most *minerals* found?
3   What other word(s) could you use instead of *gleam?*

*roughneck oilman

4 Explain the meaning of *raw meat*.
5 What does *gradually* mean?
6 What happens when water *freezes* and ice *melts*?
7 What is the meaning of *the cold is unbelievable*?
8 Explain: 'the pipeline will *cost a fortune*'.
9 What does Mark Grigson mean when he says: 'You'd be *done for*'?

*done for** in danger

Canada's ice and snow

B   Questions

1   What crops do the Canadians grow on the prairies, and what grows between the prairies and the Arctic North?
2   What is the name for the land which lies between the last trees and the Arctic Ocean? What happens to it in winter?
3   Why do the Eskimos prefer to be called the 'Inuit'?
4   The Inuit used to be nomads. Describe how they lived.
5   What do the Inuit do in the towns the government has built for them?
6   Why can't the pilots in the Arctic use a compass?
7   Why mustn't roughnecks in the Arctic take hold of anything made of iron or steel without wearing a glove?

C   Grammar

These adverbs or adverbial phrases are in the text. Put them into sentences, or a short passage, about your everyday life.

bitterly — cheerfully — a great deal — gradually — very often — once more — again — any longer/no longer — still — after a while

D   Function

Sympathy

Plane crashed on landing, everybody killed immediately. Young scientist, Bill, on board. He had been married for only 10 months. His wife so upset she doesn't wish to see anyone.

Use these notes and the phrases below to make up a dialogue between Tom, who knew Bill, and his friend Jean. Lengthen the dialogue if you wish.

I'm terribly sorry. — It really is awful. — At least they didn't feel any pain. — He was so young. — How terrible for his wife! — What a waste! — I can understand how she feels. — Is there anything I can do for her?

14 The Canadian sportsman, odd man out?

Canada has not done as well at international sport as the other Dominions in the Commonwealth of Nations. One cause may be the climate. Canadian athletes must find it difficult to train during the long, cold winters. Perhaps that's why they win few medals at the Commonwealth and Olympic Games. As for other Commonwealth sports, such as cricket and rugby, they are minor sports in Canada. Canadian football is like American football, but not quite, so American and Canadian teams never play each other. The Canadians play baseball, but their professional teams belong to the American leagues. They do not often play international matches.

'You just don't understand!' Suzie said crossly to her English cousin, Sam. 'You're suggesting that we're no good at anything, because we don't very often get our name on the sporting pages of the world's newspapers. Do you really think it's so important to be famous for beating other countries? You ought to be here when the big freeze starts. We have water everywhere—lakes, pools, rivers, and they always freeze and stay frozen right through the winter. When it snows, we just brush the snow away so, you see, we have natural skating rinks in every town and city, and the sun shines nearly all the time. It's very cold, of course, but the cold doesn't worry you if you wear gloves and a woolly cap to cover your ears. Everybody can skate in Canada. You should see tiny kids learning to skate and falling on their bottoms!'

'But doesn't it give kids ambitions, skating so well?' asked Sam. 'Like English kids kicking a football about?'

'Yes, it does. When they're old enough, the kids come out with sticks and play hockey. Then, if a boy starts playing really well, he might get noticed and be given the chance of playing in a professional team. Hockey – what you call 'ice hockey' – is the sport Canadians usually enjoy playing most. There are about twelve teams in this part of North America—three Canadian teams and the rest in the USA.'

'So the Americans . . . ?'

'No!' Suzie interrupted. 'The players in the US teams are

95% Canadian. When the Chicago Blackhawks play the Toronto Maple Leafs, the crowd shouts and cheers throughout the game. You said the other day you thought the Canadians were a quiet, serious people. You wouldn't think so if you went to a hockey game at the Maple Leaf arena! It's the most violent game there is, and we all love it and cheer on the Maple Leafs!'

'What do you mean, 'violent'?' asked Sam.

'Well, they play it at a very great speed. It is supposed to be the fastest game in the world. Players reach speeds of more than 50 km an hour. Their bodies are protected with thick padding, but when they crash into each other, they often start fighting and hitting each other with their sticks. Players who start a fight get sent to the penalty box to cool off for a while. Being hit by the puck is no joke, either. It can speed across the ice at 160 km an hour, and sometimes it travels through the air. That can be dangerous.'

'But your international team isn't too good. It never seems to win a gold medal at the Olympics,' Sam said.

'That's because our best team is professional, and so it can't take part in the Olympics.'

'Doesn't your top professional team play other international teams?'

'Not often,' said Suzie, 'but Canada and the USSR played a series of eight games recently. We only just won—by four games to three, with one tied. That wasn't bad when you consider Russia's population, and the Russian climate is like ours, only worse! Still, it was a shock.'

'Do the French Canadians play?'

'Of course. They have a very good team, the Montreal Canadians.'

● ● ● ● ● ● ● ● ● ● ● ● ● ● ● ● ● ● ● ●

There is a Canadian game, a really ancient game invented by the Indians many centuries ago. It is played with a stick bent at the end, where there's a small net. The ball is carried in this net and thrown from one player to another. The French called it 'lacrosse', because the stick looked like a crozier, the curved stick carried by a bishop. The Indians called it 'the little brother of war'! The goals were several miles apart and there were hundreds, sometimes thousands, of players on each side, who tried to knock out as many of the other side as possible, so as to leave a clear path to the goal. The winning side left a trail of injured warriors behind it. It was a way of testing a man's courage and skill.

The modern team has 12 players, but it is still a rough game. It is quite fair to knock a man over with your stick. Lacrosse is called Canada's national game, but today far more men play ice hockey. Lacrosse is more popular with women and is played in many girls' schools in Canada, the USA, Britain and Ireland. Women may knock the ball out of an opponent's stick, but body blows and violence of any kind are strictly forbidden.

A   Vocabulary

1   What makes a *climate*?
2   Give an example of an *international match*.
3   What does *beating other countries* mean?
4   What is a *rink*?
5   What is the opposite of a) a *quiet, serious* people b) *at full speed*?
6   What is the meaning of: *Being hit by the puck is no joke*?
7   What is an *injured warrior*?

B   Questions

1   Why is it difficult for Canadian athletes to train during winter?
2   What do Canadians do when the big freeze starts?
3   What do people who are learning to skate often do?
4   What might be the ambition of a Canadian boy who skates very well?
5   When do hockey players get sent to the penalty box?
6   In what way was the Indian game violent?
7   Which is the more popular game in Canada, lacrosse or hockey?

C   Translation or interpreting

Find the last but one paragraph in the Unit, beginning 'There is a Canadian game ... man's courage and skill'. Either translate it, or act as an interpreter, giving the general meaning of the passage in your own language.

D   Function

Making an accusation and showing anger

> You kicked me deliberately. — It was *not* my fault. — No, he wont'! — It was *not* a mistake. — That's complete nonsense. — Don't try to make excuses. — You kicked me from behind. — All right! I'll go to Mr Bellis. He'll know who's telling the truth. — Yes, he will! — It was a mistake.

Invent a dialogue between Gene and Rick, two young footballers.

Gene   You kicked me deliberately!
Rick   No, I didn't. You ran into me. It was your fault!

Now carry on.

15   Canadian English—how different is it from American?

'What part of the States do you come from?'
  'I'm not American. I'm Canadian.'
  This is a mistake that Europeans often make. Many Americans, too, admit that it takes them a while to tell if it's an American talking or a Canadian. This upsets some Canadians, because they want people to recognise them as

Canadians. They want everyone to know that Canada is an independent nation with its own special character.

American English was probably brought to Canada by the Loyalists who fled there during the Revolutionary War (1776–83), for even as late as 1813, 80% of all British Canadians had come from the USA.

From the very first, Canada was a country with two languages, neither of which influenced the other very much, because the French and British spoke to each other so little. Canadian English has always remained very like American English, and the influence of the Indian and Inuit languages was no greater than the influence of French. But here are some important words that have found their way via Canadian dictionaries into British dictionaries:

Canadian word of French origin	**French meaning**
prairies (great plains of Canada)	from *prairie*, meadow
crevasse	wide, deep crack in ice
rapids	from *rapide*, river flowing fast over rocks
cache	secret place for hiding something
mush! (command to a dog)	from *marche!*, get going! be off with you!
canoe	from *canoë*, light boat moved by paddles
butte	steep hill rising straight out of a plain
portage	from *porter*, to carry; carrying of a canoe overland past rapids
caribou (Canadian reindeer)	the French word *caribou* probably came from an Indian word

Air Canada the title of the Canadian airline is a French construction, like *Air France*, though there are airlines which have the same construction—*Air India*

words of Indian origin.

moose, gopher,	animals
chipmunk, skunk	(**American** Indian *segongue*)
tomahawk	Indian axe (Australians too sometimes use this work instead of 'hatchet')
wigwam	Indian tent
mocassin	shoe of soft leather
pemmican	dried meat, pressed into small pieces so that it can be carried on long journeys
muskeg	boggy kind of country in north of Canada
toboggan	light sleigh used by Canadian Indians for carrying loads over snow, from French Canadian *tabaggane*, taken from the Algonquin Indian word *tobokun*

Some of these words of Indian origin may have been known to the Loyalists before they settled in Canada.

words of Inuit origin.

kayak	Inuit canoe
anorak	waterproof jacket
husky	sleigh dog of the Inuit, from Inuit word *huskinani*

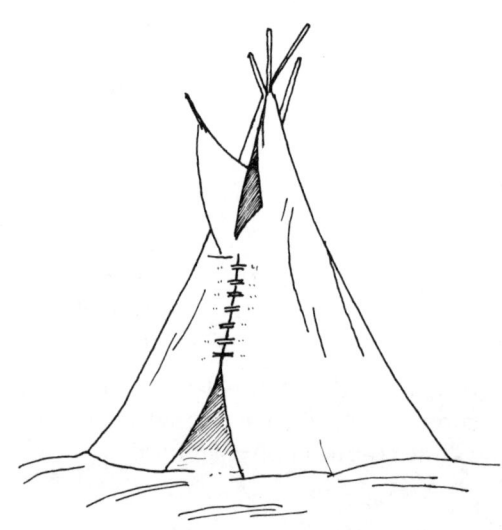

words said to have originated in Canada

hooch	slang word for strong alcoholic drink
bobsled	two short sleighs joined together to carry logs
Johnny Canuck	slang for a Canadian (any Canadian)
Jean Baptiste	slang for a French Canadian

There are not many regional dialects in Canada, though the people in the Maritime provinces speak an English that is closer to British English than anywhere else in the country except British Columbia, where elderly British couples often retire. Most words concerned with government are British English rather than American English: Parliament, constituency, poll, House of Commons, Prime Minister, etc. There are also British words which some Canadians prefer to the words Americans use:

British	**American**
blinds	*shades*
counterpane	*bedspread* (the British use either word)
cupboard	*closet*
holiday	*vacation* (British university students use *vacation*)
odd jobs	*chores* (the British frequently use *chores*)
staircase	*stairway* (Americans also use *staircase*)
tap	*faucet*
drain (inside house)	*sewerage*
bush	in the sense of uncultivated, tree-covered land, a word also used in Australia, New Zealand and South Africa, but not the USA

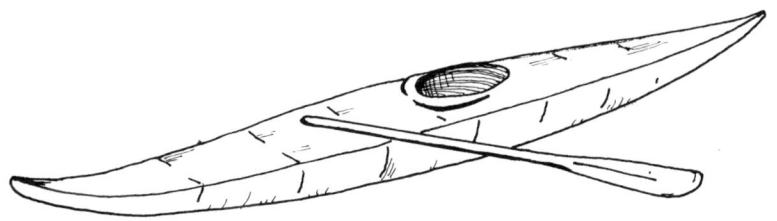

A   Vocabulary

1   Put *recognise* into a sentence of your own to show you understand what it means.
2   When you try and *influence* someone, what do you hope will happen?
3   Show that you understand the meaning of *character* (page 81, line 2)
4   What are *dictionaries* used for?
5   Which of the words of French Canadian, Indian and Inuit origin are used in your language? Has the spelling been altered?
6   Explain what is meant by *regional*.
7   *Couple* can be used with almost any noun, for people, animals, objects. How many are there in a couple?

B   Questions

1   Do Americans recognise the Canadian accent at once?
2   Where did Canadian English probably come from?
3   Why hasn't the French language influenced Canadian English much?
4   Can you think of any other airlines whose name is formed in the same way as *Air Canada* and *Air France*?
5   Why are most words concerned with the Canadian government in British rather than American English?

C   Grammar

Present conditional, perfect conditional

Turn the verbs in brackets into the correct conditional tense.

Example   I *would help* you, if I was strong enough.
             I *would have helped* you, if I had had time.

1   If the river had more water, I (paddle) down it in my canoe.

2   If he went to Canada, he (fly) Air Canada.
3   I'm sure you (be able) to tell the difference between a kayak and a canoe.
4   I (pull down) the blinds if I wanted to keep out the sun.
5   They (not lose) all their clothes, if they had locked the cupboard.
6   We (not dream) of lending you our toboggan. You (smash) it.
7   She (see) plenty of moose if she had gone to Canada.

D   Function

Disappointment

You failed to get a job in Montreal because your French wasn't good enough.

I was bitterly disappointed. — I really was expecting to get the job. — No, I'm so miserable, I can't ... — When he told me, I could hardly believe it. — I feel like jumping in the St Lawrence!

Friend   You didn't really think you'd get the job, did you?
You   I certainly did, ...
Friend   You really minded?
You   Yes ...
Friend   So it was a real shock?
You   Yes, it was ...
Friend   Have you any other plans?
You   ... I ... !

Australasia

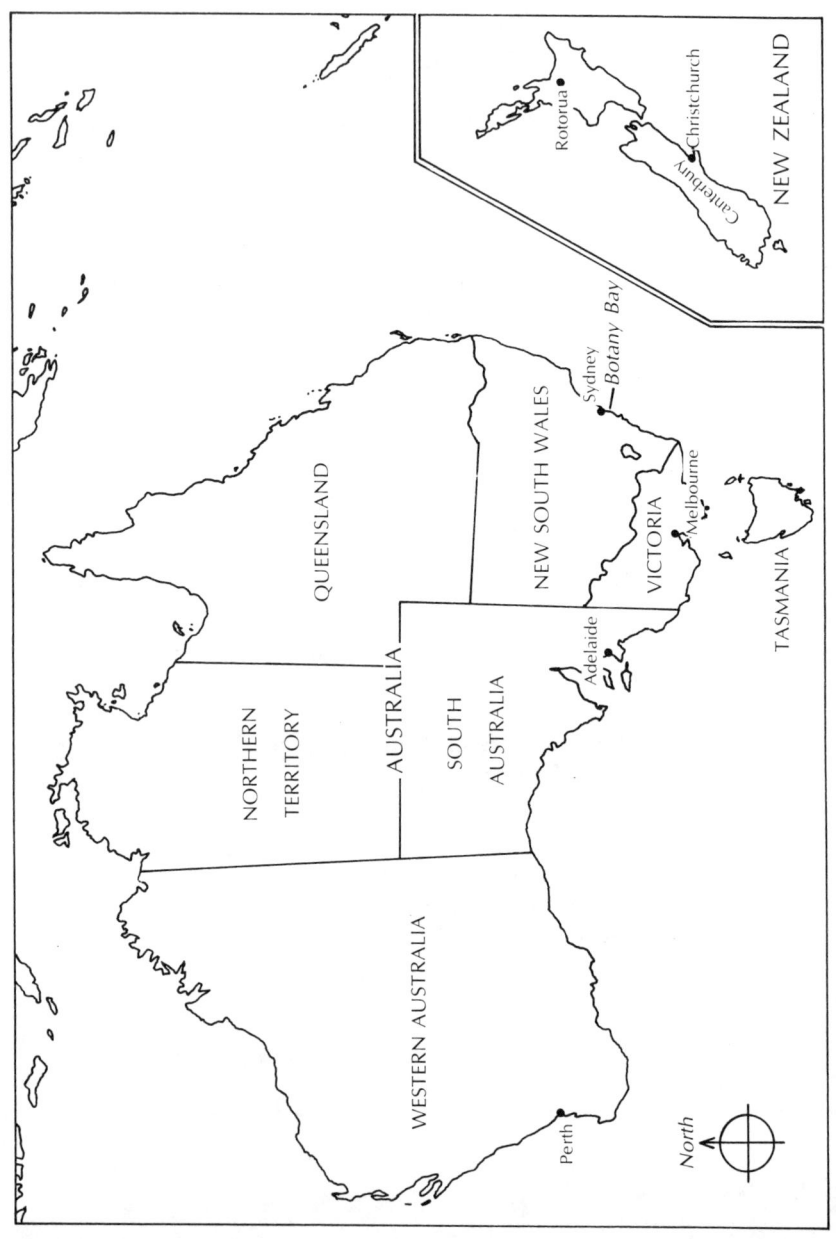

16   The Discovery of Australia and New Zealand

Australia and New Zealand were discovered in 1642 by the Dutch explorer, Tasman, but for more than a hundred years after that they remained vague lines on the map. It was thought that they were part of a Great South Land in which civilised human beings lived. Scientists in Britain were anxious to find out if this land really did exist, so in 1768 they sent an expedition to the southern seas to look for it. The leader of the expedition was Captain James Cook of the Royal Navy, one of the greatest explorers of all time. He took with him on board his ship, *Endeavour*, scientists and artists whose job it was to make a record of all the strange things they might discover on the voyage. Cook never did discover the mysterious South Land, but far down in the southern ocean he *did* discover the east coast of New Zealand, and he raised the Union Jack to claim it for Britain. He then sailed right round the two islands, making maps of the whole coast and naming mountains and bays and islands, which still bear the same names today.

Cook and his companions came face to face with the Maoris, the native people who had come to New Zealand from the South Pacific Islands in the 14th century. They were more warlike than the South Sea Islanders. One sailor returned white-faced and trembling from a trip ashore. 'What be the matter with you, Master Simkins?' asked a shipmate. 'The matter! I see'd one o' them savages gnawing a roasted forearm!'

After leaving New Zealand, Cook sailed north west. He believed that with luck he might find another land, and nineteen days later, that is exactly what he did. It was Australia. They landed in a bay on the north east coast which is today part of Sydney, and to their astonishment they saw plants and creatures that no white man had ever seen before: kangaroos and wombats and koalas, brilliantly coloured birds and butterflies, and grey-green eucalyptus trees of all kinds. Cook named the place 'Botany Bay'. They also met the dark-skinned Aborigines. The crew were scornful of them and called them animals, but Cook admired their simple way of life. He wrote in his diary: 'With all our possessions and comfortable way of life, we do not seem as

Captain Cook's arrival at Botany Bay

happy as they are.' He realised what would happen to them one day, and he was saddened.

Ten years later, Australia's first settlers landed in Sydney Harbour, which was only a few miles up the coast from Botany Bay. Captain Arthur Phillip, the commander of the little fleet, wrote: 'We had the satisfaction of finding the finest harbour in the world.' Not many people would disagree with him today. These first settlers were convicts, women as well as men, who had been sent to this wild land as a punishment. There were also soldiers to guard them. Only 10% of Australians are descended from convicts, most of whom were not really criminals. There were rebellious Irishmen, English labourers who had formed unlawful trade unions, girls who had stolen half a loaf of bread for their starving children.

By 1823 there were only about 30,000 settlers in Sydney, but gradually Australia took shape. By 1840 the borders of six separate colonies had been decided. These colonies stretched right round the coast from Queensland in the north east to Western Australia in the far south west. But to begin with the colonists had very little say in governing themselves. Each colony was ruled by a governor appointed by the British Government. The Australians, who have never liked being told what to do, particularly by upper class 'Poms', (the Australian nickname for the English), demanded self-rule, and they got it, for the British had not forgotten how they lost the American colonies. In 1901 the six colonies formed a

HINDMARSH

HERE
AT HOLDFAST BAY
LANDED THE
PIONEER SETTLERS
AND
GOVERNOR HINDMARSH
ANNOUNCED THE
ESTABLISHMENT OF
THE GOVERNMENT
ON DEC. 28TH 1836

confederation of states which was called the Commonwealth of Australia.

The exploration of the vast unknown continent went on throughout the 19th century. In 1803 Matthew Flinders sailed right round Australia, noting how bare and uninviting most of the coast was. Then two explorers broke through the great mountain wall which runs all the way down the east coast, and discovered the outback, which stretches inland and west for hundreds of miles, getting drier and drier until it becomes waterless desert.

New Zealand was colonised much later. In fact, it might never have been colonised by Britain at all if it hadn't been for the 'old enemy', France, who had plans to use it as a settlement for French convicts. The first colony of British settlers did not arrive until 1840, and twelve years later they were given self-rule. Like Australia, New Zealand became an independent country within the British Commonwealth and Empire.

A   Vocabulary

1   What is a *vague* line?
2   Describe a *bay*.
3   If you go *ashore*, where do you come from?
4   What is a *creature*?
5   What comes into a *harbour*?
6   Give the meaning of *convict*.
7   What things often make people *rebellious*?
8   What is the meaning of *bare* land?

B   Questions

1   Did the Great South Land exist?
2   What did Cook do as he sailed round the two islands of New Zealand?
3   Why was the sailor afraid after his trip ashore?
4   Why did Cook call the landing place 'Botany Bay'?
5   What did Cook think would happen to the Aborigines?

6   How were the Governors of the colonies chosen?
7   What is self-rule?

C   Grammar

The future tense

Take the paragraph beginning, 'By 1823 there were only . . .', and turn it into the future. But be careful! Two verbs should not be changed, and two should be changed to the future perfect.

By 1823 there *will only be* about 30,000 settlers . . .

D   Function

Answering questions

Yes, I am, have, do. (etc) — No, I'm not, haven't, don't. (etc).
Yes, I was, had, did. (etc) — No, I wasn't, hadn't, didn't. (etc).
Yes, I would. — No I wouldn't. — Yes, there were. — No, there weren't.

If you say 'No', add the correct answer.
Example Q Did Cook discover New Zealand?
    A No, he didn't. Tasman did.

1 *Q* Do the Maoris live in Australia?
2 *Q* Did Cook sail right round New Zealand?
3 *Q* Were the first Australian settlers convicts?
4 *Q* Is there a bridge across Sydney Harbour?
5 *Q* Have you ever seen a picture of this bridge?
6 *Q* Have you ever been to Australia?
7 *Q* Would you like to go to Australia?
8 *Q* Do the New Zealanders call the British 'Poms'?
9 *Q* Were there 12 colonies in Australia?
10 *Q* Did the French colonise New Zealand?

17 People and government

It happens in history that conquerors sometimes destroy whole peoples in their empires. The British killed every single Aborigine in the Australian island of Tasmania. But in New Zealand, although there were fierce battles, the British and the Maoris had a respect for one another. The fighting stopped, and before long Maoris and whites began to intermarry. Today the Maoris have equal rights with the whites, but they still do not always have equal opportunities.

The Treaty of Waitangi signed by the British and the Maoris

The Aborigines of Australia – there are some 160,000 of them – have a more ancient and simple way of life than the Maoris. Nobody knows where they came from, or when. They once wandered freely over the vast continent, of which they were the only inhabitants. Now some live in reserves, away from white people. Others work on sheep stations (ranches), but the rest have moved into towns, where they live in awful poverty, unemployed and uneducated. However, most Australians now agree that the Aborigines have been cruelly neglected, and that they have just the same right to a good life as white Australians.

Some views on the Australians

Here are some common views that the British have of Australians. Some Australians would agree, others might not. They are fiercely independent and they say exactly what they think, even if it sometimes sounds rude. The sharp-faced, leathery-skinned horseman rounding up his flocks of sheep is typical only of the men who work in the outback. Five out of six Australians live in the suburbs (called 'slurbs') of towns and cities, and they like to own the house they live in. It is still sometimes said that Australia is not a place for women, and some men still like to spend more time with their mates than with their wives. But more and more Australians have wider interests, now that Australia has citizens from so many different countries. Since World War 2, nearly 4,000,000 immigrants from 120 countries have settled in Australia, and the population has risen from 7,500,000 in 1945 to 15,400,000 in 1980. Sydney has 3,500,000 inhabitants, Melbourne 3,000,000. Australians now take a much greater interest in the Arts.

Australians demand 'fair-goes' (fair treatment), not only for themselves, but also for their mates. Loyalty to their mates is of great importance to them, more important than obeying rules. They work to earn enough to enjoy themselves, preferably out of doors. Some Aussie men pride themselves on being 'macho' (very masculine), and fights in pubs are not uncommon. They tend to be carefree. An Aussie flying to London in the middle of a 'down-under' summer, arrived at Heathrow in a snow storm, wearing only an open neck shirt and a pair of shorts.

New Zealanders are tough, too, but less lively and less carefree. They live just as comfortably, and they have one of the best welfare systems in the world. Hospital treatment costs patients nothing at all.

The Australians are becoming more and more attracted towards the USA, but not the New Zealanders, who do not have much love for the Americans. Both Australians and New Zealanders, especially the younger ones, have a great pride in their own countries. They no longer have strong ties with the mother country.

Australia has been criticised for refusing to accept non-white immigrants, but she has allowed in a large number of Vietnamese refugees. Since 1945, New Zealand has accepted many Polynesians from the Pacific Islands.

Government

Like the USA, Australia is a federation of states, but both federal and state governments are run on British, not American lines. Australian members of Parliament are elected by proportional representation (see p 19). Everyone aged 18 and over has to vote in federal and state elections. Anyone who does not bother to vote has to pay a fine. There are two main parties, Labour, a middle-of-the-road socialist party, and the Liberal Party, which stands for free enterprise.

The New Zealand Parliament has only one House, which it calls the House of Representatives. Otherwise the whole New Zealand parliamentary system is very like that of the UK. There are two parties, the Labour Party and the National Party, which is a conservative welfare party. The Queen is head of both the Australian and the New Zealand governments, but is represented in both cases by a Governor-General.

A　Vocabulary

1　What do *conquerors* do?
2　Can you think of any other words for *vast*?
3　Why are there *reserves* for the Aborigines? What is a reserve?
4　Give an example of someone being *rude*.
5　What other word, or words, have the meaning of *mates*? (page 93, line 10)
6　Where do you usually find a *patient*?
7　What is a *middle-of-the-road* political party?

B　Questions

1　What differences are there between the Aborigines and the Maoris?
2　What do many Australians in the outback do?
3　What is more important to an Australian than obeying rules?
4　Do you remember the Australian who arrived at Heathrow in shorts and a shirt? What mistake did he make?
5　At what age can you vote a) in Australia b) in your country?
6　In Canada the colonies became 'provinces'. What did they become in Australia?
7　Give some examples of 'welfare' in a modern state.

C   Grammar

Here are some adjectives used in the text. Use them in sentences of your own.

whole — single — simple — fierce — equal — ancient — awful — common — uncommon — typical — tough

D   Function

Answering an accusation

Nothing! — You won't believe me, but it's true. — You're quite right. I did. — Good idea, but why don't you look in your handbag first? — That's very unfair. There are probably fewer thieves here than in England.

Use the phrases above to fill in the following dialogue.

Englishwoman   I saw you put your hand in my bag!
Australian   . . .
Englishwoman   I was always afraid that Australians were thieves.
Australian   . . .
Englishwoman   What were you going to take from my bag?
Australian   . . .
Englishwoman   I think I'll call a policeman.
Australian   . . .
(The Englishwoman finds a printed sheet in her bag which says: 'Welcome to Australia! Dine at the Wallaby Steak House.')

From an advertisement for aboriginal art:
"Full refund if not delighted. Our boomerangs always come back".
(Peterborough, The Daily Telegraph)

A roundabout at an English fair

An English shopping centre

Reconstructing England's past

The wild mountain country which kept Scotland free for so long

Backpackers on a US mountain trail

Autumn colours in the Guadaloupe National Park, Texas

Desert which the early pioneers of America had to cross

An Eskimo carving soapstone

A Canadian cowboy
shows off his skill

Volcano, Mt Ngauruhoe, New Zealand

Picking kiwi fruit in New Zealand

Preparing for an Aborigine festival, Australia

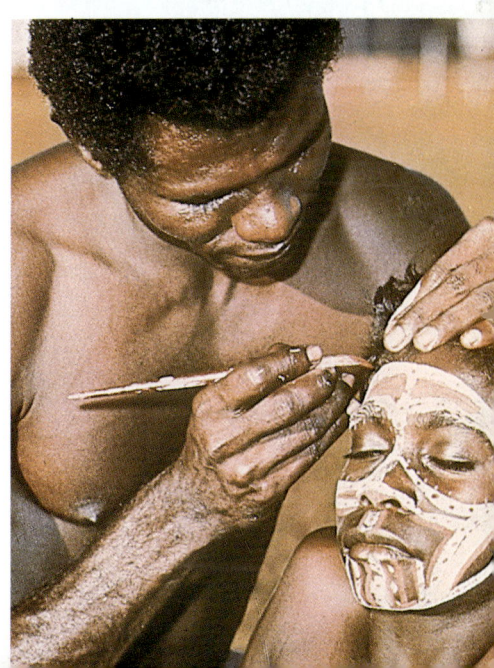

View from a Caribbean hotel

Caribbean Carnival

Mountains and gardens on the Caribbean island of St Lucia

The Emir of Kano's trumpeters, Nigeria

At the Salah festival, Nigeria

Modern architecture, Kenya

Traditional houses, Kenya

Gareth Williams stopped off at Perth, capital of Western Australia, to visit his uncle, Phil Edwards, who was a doctor with the Royal Doctors' Flying Service. The Flying Service has saved many lives in the outback.

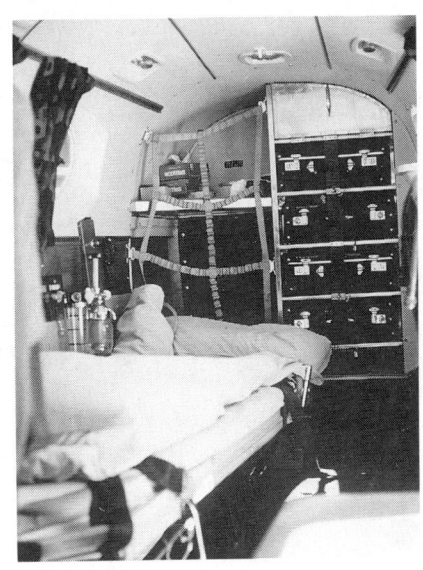

The small corner of Western Australia where most people live is like a huge oasis, with the Indian Ocean on two sides and the endless desert on the other two. Perth's nearest neighbour, Adelaide, is over 2,600 km away, and between them lies the vast Nullabor Plain, which is dead flat and without a tree for 800 km. Yet along the coast on either side of Perth, Gareth was amazed by the variety of crops and plantations.

His uncle drove him through forests of huge eucalyptus trees, whose wood is so hard that it can be used for underwater posts. Further up the coast, they stopped in a vast plantation of fruit trees. There was every kind of tree, from bananas and mangoes to oranges and lemons, and there were vegetable gardens, too, in which a small black-haired man was hard at work. Phil called to him: 'Alberto!

Come and explain to my Welsh nephew what has made the desert flower.'

'Well, we found water and brought it to the crops—irrigated them, in fact. There's a river which floods and then dries up. Now we catch the flood water and store it, and we've found water under the sand, too.'

'Are you getting on better with your neighbours?' asked Phil.

'They still say, "You work too hard, Alberto. It's not fair-goes!"'

They drove on through wheatfields. 'We export a lot of wheat, you know, Gareth,' said Phil. 'We used to export it to Britain, but now it's China. We've turned our faces to the east. Odd, isn't it, when you come to think of it? But Australia is an exciting country to live in. We're gradually discovering that more of it is fit to live in than we'd thought. Take the Kimberly Range, up north. They've changed the course of the river and turned the land into cattle country.'

'I suppose you still export a lot of wool?' asked Gareth.

'My goodness, yes! Do you know how many sheep we've got, scattered all over the continent? 135,000,000! That's about 14% of all the sheep in the world, and they give us the softest wool anyone could want. There's such a demand for our wool, laddie, that we export 90% of it, and that's a world record! Australians raise cattle, too, you know, lots of 'em, and we sell most of our beef and veal to the USA.'

One day Phil got a call from an iron ore mine. A miner had had a bad heart attack. Gareth went with him. They were soon flying low over the desert. Below them a black metalled road cut straight through the red earth with hardly a bend. Dirt roads branched off it, leading to broken-down huts and ruined mine shafts.

'I was called out here once,' Phil said, pointing. 'Had to go into that shaft down there. Old man had gone crazy and killed himself because he couldn't find any gold.'

Soon a range of mountains appeared, rust-red humps, none of them much more than 1200 metres high. 'The Hammersley Range,' Phil said. 'Once we thought all the plateau was barren and useless. Now we know there's enough iron ore in those mountains to keep the world supplied for a hundred years.'

'What do they do with the ore?' asked Gareth. 'Load it as it is?'

'No, first it's broken up on the spot, then it's carried 500 km by rail down to Port Hedland or Dampier. From there it's shipped straight to Japan. Japan's the big market for all our ores, especially bauxite (from which aluminium comes)— we're the world's biggest producer of bauxite, and we export nickel and zinc, and Heaven knows what other minerals. And we've more coal than we need. So we export what's left—to Japan.'

Gareth grinned. 'They call you the lucky country. I can see why!'

'They're right! Off Barrow Island there are scores of oil rigs. In 1960 we didn't know we had any oil. Now we produce almost as much as we need—and we've got natural gas, too.'

They picked up the sick man and flew him back to Perth, where he was rushed to one of the city's public health hospitals.

New Zealand

Every British housewife has bought New Zealand butter, or seen it in supermarkets, and Canterbury lamb is the next best thing to home-grown lamb—and much cheaper, too. The Canterbury plains, on South Island, are famous for their sheep. New Zealand also exports a lot of wool and has turned, like Australia, to the Far East for markets. From the timber of her great forests, her paper-mills make paper for export to Japan. New Zealand has no oil and very little coal, but she has plenty of natural water power and has built a number of hydro-electric dams.

Reproduced by kind permission of Newlands, Knight & Round Limited, London.

The kiwi is New Zealand's national bird

A   Vocabulary

1   What is the meaning of *dead flat*?
2   What does *variety* mean?
3   Explain the verb *irrigate*.
4   What can you make with *wool*?
5   What animals do *beef* and *veal* come from?
6   What is the opposite of a *road with bends*?
7   Why is *barren* land *useless*?

B   Questions

1   What surrounds Western Australia?
2   Why can the wood of the eucalyptus tree be used for underwater posts?
3   How do they use water from the floods?
4   Where did the Western Australians once export their wheat?
5   How much of their wool do Australians keep for themselves?
6   What do they do with the iron ore before they send it to the port?
7   Why is New Zealand lamb often called 'Canterbury lamb'?
8   Where does a lot of New Zealand's electric power come from?

C   Grammar

Make up short sentences of your own, using the following prepositions.

between — through — without — along — under — all over — into — like

Example. The road goes between two mountains.

D   Function

Help! A boy has fallen off his horse on a lonely sheep station in the outback. His mother phones the flying doctor.

Fill in the gaps, using the following phrases.
Is there any other doctor who could come sooner? — Please hurry! — Please tell us what we should do. — We're very worried. — How soon can you get here? — Please come quickly, doctor.

Mother	My son has had an accident ...
Doctor	What's the matter with him?
Mother	It's his head. He fell off his horse ...
Doctor	Is he unconscious?
Mother	Yes ...
Doctor	Not before five o'clock, I'm afraid.
Mother	Oh, dear! ...
Doctor	No, I'm sorry, there isn't.
Mother	... while we wait?
Doctor	Just keep him warm. Don't move him.

19   Enjoying oneself Down Under

Eastern Australia, where most Australians live, has two frontiers. There is the vast South Pacific Ocean and inland, beyond the mountains, there is the vast desert of the outback. The bush, on the edge of the desert, is the most exciting part of the outback, with its slender, papery-barked eucalyptus trees and yellow-flowered wattle, the sun shining through the grey-green leaves, and the blackened stumps of past fires. At times the heat of the midday sun sets fire to the bush, and flames roar through the dry scrub, threatening outback towns and sheep stations. But on the seaward side of the mountains the climate is pleasant, sub-tropical in

Queensland, while in New South Wales and Victoria there's a nip in the air in winter, though the sun shines most of the time throughout the whole year.

Mark Odell, a Sydney bank clerk, has never been to the outback. Few Australians have. Mark is married with two young children and lives in his own small house overlooking Botany Bay. His garden just has room for a hard tennis court. The suburbs of Sydney are full of private tennis courts, since they are cheap to build. Most sports in Australia are cheap. For instance, anyone can play golf. There are no expensive clubs as in Britain. Australians strongly disapprove of special advantages for the rich. In the evening Mark likes, once or twice a week, to meet his mates at the pub. His wife, Jean, goes to the opera whenever she can. Some people claim that the Sydney Opera House is the most exciting place in the world for listening to music. All the great orchestras and opera singers visit Sydney and Melbourne.

Sydney Opera House

Thanks to the climate, Mark and his family can be out of doors summer and winter. At winter weekends, he and Jean go up into the mountains to ski. Alongside a jetty in Sydney Harbour there is a small yacht which Mark shares with three mates. At weekends the harbour is crowded with sailing boats, large and small. The Australians are fine yachtsmen. Their greatest success was winning back in 1983 the America's Cup, which the Americans had held since 1851.

In summer, as soon as the day's work is over, the whole Odell family go off to the beach to 'sunbake'[1] and swim and go surfing. Mark is an expert surfer and enjoys taking risks and riding the tops of the great waves. Jean was a champion swimmer when she was sixteen. Australians have won a number of Olympic and Commonwealth gold medals for swimming. They have also produced several world-class runners. Each city has a number of small stadiums where athletes can train without cost.

Jean often takes her young son to one of the many concrete cricket pitches in the parks, and bowls to him with a tennis ball. Cricket is the national sport. Rivalry with the English goes back a hundred years. Australia has so far won more Test Matches than England. Recently the Australians had a tigerish fast bowler. As he ran up to bowl, the crowd cried, 'Kill, kill, kill!' The Aussies are not at all pleased when they lose a Test Match. Betting on horses, or anything else, is another popular pastime.

The New Zealand climate is mild, so New Zealanders, like Australians, can spend most of their free time out of doors. It is a mountainous country, with many peaks over 2000 metres, and streams rush down the steep slopes. Trout, brought from England, have been very successful in New Zealand, and anyone can fish for them. 'When I was in England,' Len Meade of Christchurch told his English cousin, Bob, 'I had to pay the owner of a stream £20 a day for the right to fish. I didn't even see a trout! I told him he could keep his fish!'

'Don't miss Rotorua,' Len told his cousin. 'It's wonderful! It's got geysers and hot springs. You can have a hot bath, if you feel like it, and you'll have Maori guides ... Yes, the

A geyser at Rotorua

volcanoes round about are active ... Nothing to worry about! They won't erupt! Of course, there's always the chance of an earthquake! The last big one was in 1931 ... Yes, it destroyed Napier completely.'

The broad chain of mountains which run all the way down the west coast of South Island have fine skiing slopes and splendid trails for hikers in summer. In the far south there are tall mountains and forests which have now been made into a national park, and there are great cliffs dropping straight down to the inky black waters of the narrow sounds, which are like Norwegian fjords, only much more wild and lonely.

New Zealanders play the same sports as Australians, but their national sport, rugby, is more than a game, for winning is a matter of national pride. The New Zealand team is called 'The All Blacks' – they wear black shirts and shorts – and they are usually all-conquering.

1 sunbathe

A   Vocabulary

1   What is a *stump*? Why are stumps often blackened in the Australian bush?
2   What does a *nip in the air* suggest?
3   What would most people say instead of *sunbake*?
4   What may happen if you *take risks*?
5   What do you think the meaning of *tigerish* is here?
6   What is a *sound* here?

B   Questions

1   What can sometimes happen when there is a bush fire?
2   What is there in the Odell family's garden?
3   Why can anyone play golf in Sydney?
4   Why can Mark and his family spend so much time out of doors?
5   When you are surfing, what carries you to the beach?
6   Where did the trout in New Zealand come from?
7   Why is it possible to have a hot bath in Rotorua?
8   Who are the All Blacks?

C   Grammar

Purpose

Why do you do it?
I do it to earn some money
        or in order to earn some money
        or so that I can earn some money.

1   Why do Mark and Jean go into the mountains in the winter?
2   Why do the Odell family go to the beach in summer?
3   Why do athletes go to the stadium?
4   Why does Mark swim out to sea?
5   Why do some people go to Rotorua?

D Function

Apology

You are a New Zealander and you are fishing in an English trout stream when the owner catches you. You use the following phrases.

I'm terribly sorry. — I'm afraid I never saw it. — Oh, yes, I see it now. It really was very careless of me. — No, I'm afraid I didn't know. — Please forgive me. — Please accept my apologies.

Owner	Can't you see that notice—'Fishing Private'?
New Zealander	. . .
Owner	Over there, on the other bank.
New Zealander	. . .
Owner	Well, what have you to say for yourself? Don't you know you always have to pay for the right to fish?
New Zealander	. . . You see, I'm a New Zealander.
Owner	Can I have your word that you won't fish here again?
New Zealander	There aren't any fish, anyway. But . . .

A "roo guard" as protection against a kangaroo

20 The language Down Under

'Emma Chizzit?'

The shop assistant looked bewildered. 'I'm afraid you've got the wrong person. I'm Susan Brown.'

'OK, Susan! Don't yer tike the micky owt o' me![1] Emma Chizzit?'

He put his hand on the model of Big Ben, and suddenly Susan understood. 'Oh, how much is it!'

Abe Connors snapped. 'That's what I said! Emma Chizzit?'

'I'm sorry. I'm afraid . . .'

Abe was getting annoyed. 'I come from Sydney, Aus-tra-lia. Where you from, Buckingham Palace?'

'Emma Chizzit' is a well-known joke about the Australian accent. Unlike Americans, many Australians don't like the English public school accent. Sometimes they make fun of it.

Australian and New Zealand speech has its origins in Cockney London. The vowel a in words like 'day', 'late', 'basin' is pronounced like the i in 'bite', ie 'di', 'lite', 'bisen' (which makes 'basin' sound exactly the same as 'bison', the American word for a buffalo). Here's a joke which is both Cockney and Australian: 'What's the difference between a buffalo and a bison?' 'I don't know. What is the difference?' 'Yer can't wash yer hands in a buffalo!'

The o in 'old' is pronounced 'owld', as in Cockney; the ending of English counties, 'He lives in Derbyshire' (etc) is pronounced -sheer instead of the standard English -sher; and the ending -ly, in 'My Sheila[2] is lovely' is pronounced 'lovelee' by both Cockneys and Australians, but 'loveli' in standard English. Australian and New Zealand accents depend on where the speakers grew up, and on their families, schools, etc. Many Australians and even more New Zealanders, speak an English which is very like British English. Some Australians deliberately exaggerate their 'Strine', particularly in the presence of 'Poms'. 'Strine' is how some Australians pronounce 'Australian' (the language).

Here are a few Australian words which are in the Oxford English Dictionary: outback; bush in its outback sense; bushranger, meaning a convict who escapes into the bush to hide and uses it as a base from which to attack and rob travellers; brumby, an unbroken (wild, untrained) horse on

KOALA
CONSERVATION
CALENDAR

1700 Millions of Koalas lived in the forests of Eastern and Southern Australia.
1916 Over 1,000,000 Koalas killed for their skins in six months.
1920 Over 2,000,000 Koala skins exported from Australia.
1922 Victorian Wildlife Authorities protected island populations of Koalas.
1923 Koalas became extinct in South Australia.
1927 In one month 600,000 Koalas were killed in Queensland.
1932 Victorian authorities released Koalas back into suitable forests as the numbers increased in island sanctuaries.
1985 Koalas have now been released into 50 localities in Victoria.

THEIR FUTURE SURVIVAL IS UP TO US!!!

an Australian sheep station; *tucker*, food eaten by hands (workers) on a sheep station; *crook*, meaning 'ill', a word much used in Australia and New Zealand; to *whinge*, an old English slang word meaning 'make a fuss', which is beginning to be used again in Britain: 'My Sheila always *whinges* when she's *crook*, but she won't go and see a doctor.'

The Australians have not changed the old Aboriginal words for animals and places, or for some of the customs which have become a part of Australian life: *koala* (bear), *kangaroo*, *wallaby* (animals); *kookaburra*, *budgerigar* (birds); *boomerang*, a hunting weapon which returns to the huntsman if he misses; *billabong*, the tributary of a river; *corroboree*, a noisy dance or party. The charming name, *Wagga-Wagga*, given to a town in New South Wales, is the Aboriginal word for the cawing of a crow; the *Murrumbridge* River means 'big water'; *Woomera*, which is a testing ground for rockets, means 'spear-throwing stick'.

New Zealanders use Maori words in the same way; *kiwi*,

the flightless bird which has become a symbol of New Zealand, just as the kangaroo and wallaby have become symbols of Australia; *Wangamu*, the North Island port, is the Maori word for 'big mouth'; *Waikete*, the longest river in New Zealand, means 'flowing water', and *Hokitika*, another river, means 'direct return'. One in eleven New Zealanders are at least half Maori, so the Maori language is having an influence on New Zealand English. One word that rugby fans know all over the world is the *Haaka*, a Maori war dance that New Zealand rugby teams perform before every international match. The object of the *Haaka* is to frighten the opposing team.

The eucalyptus tree once grew only in Australia, but has now spread all over the world. The name 'eucalyptus' was given it by one of the scientists who went with Cook on his great voyage of discovery. The Australians call it a 'gum tree'.

The English language 'down under' is being influenced by American English in the same way as it is being influenced in Britain, and for the same reasons. Australians and New Zealanders watch even more American TV programmes than the British do. They belong to the New World and their linguistic ties with the mother country are being loosened all the time.

1   Don't take the mickey out of me! (Don't make fun of me!)
2   girl (*slang*)

Wallabies

A   Vocabulary

1   How do you feel if you're *bewildered*?
2   What tone of voice does *he snapped* suggest?
3   Explain *origins*.
4   Which phrase is slang: *All right* or *OK* ?
5   Show that you understand the meaning of *to exaggerate*:
     He was exaggerating when he said that . . . . He exaggerated
     his accent so that . . .
6   If you're really *crook*, where do you go?
7   What is the name most people use for the Australian *gum
     tree*?

B   Questions

1   Why was Susan Brown bewildered?
2   Why did Abe Connors get annoyed?
3   Find a few more words that have the same vowel sound as
     'day', 'late', etc.
4   What is the slang word for the Australian language?
5   Which of the following animals, objects and places are
     found in Australia, and which in New Zealand? Do not
     look at the text: kiwi, kookaburra, boomerang, Hokitika,
     Waikete, brumby, budgerigar, Wagga-Wagga, wallaby.
     Say what they are, eg animal, bird, river, place, object.
6   When does the Haaka come to Britain?

C   Grammar

Superlatives

Examples: difficult, more difficult, *most* difficult;
good, better, *best*; happy, happier/more happy, *happiest*

What are the superlatives of the following adjectives?

bewildered — late — many — charming — direct — big —
long — noisy — lovely — few

D   Function

Making suggestions

Perhaps he was exaggerating for a joke. — Do you think you could act as interpreter? — Could you ask him to speak more slowly next time? — It was probably because of his Australian accent.

Fill in the gaps in the following dialogue.

Friend   Did you understand that Australian?
You   No, I didn't. . . .
Friend   What did you find so difficult?
You   It didn't sound like English. . . .
Friend   But his accent isn't very strong.
You   . . .
Friend   No, he wasn't joking. He wanted you to understand.
You   Well, I didn't understand a word he said. . . .

Caribbean

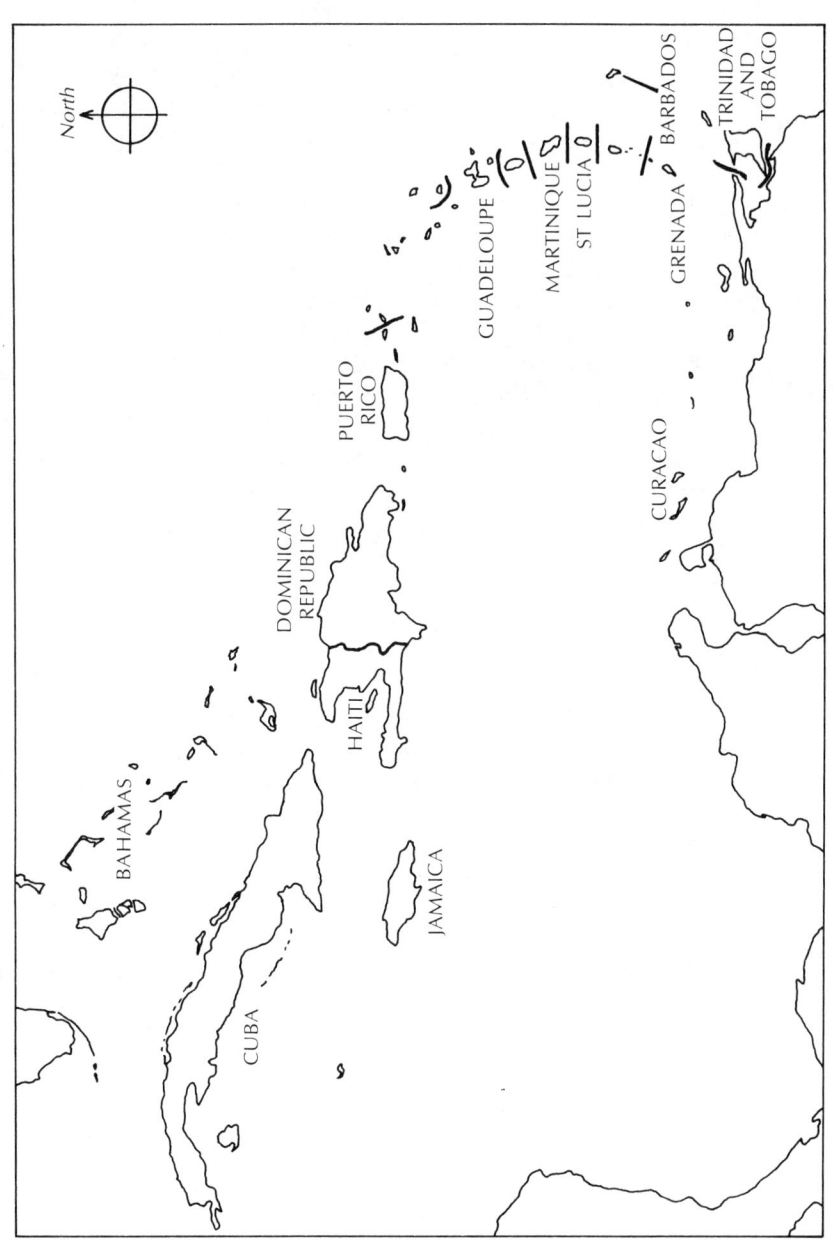

21 The islands of the Caribbean

When Christopher Columbus discovered America, his first landing was on a little island in the Bahamas. Thinking he had reached the Far East, he sailed on into the Caribbean and discovered Cuba and Hispaniola (now Haiti and the Dominican Republic). He called the natives 'Indians' and was excited to see that they wore gold rings in their noses. This awakened in the Spanish crews a great hunger for treasure, but they found none. The year was 1492.

When the Spaniards returned to the Caribbean at the end of the century they treated the 'Indians', (who were really Arawaks) with great cruelty. The Spanish horsemen hunted them for sport. There are no Arawaks left in the islands today. Before the arrival of the Spanish, the great enemies of the Arawaks were the Caribs, another 'Indian' race who came from the mainland. They, too, were almost wiped out by the Spaniards, but they gave their name to the Caribbean. The Spanish still found no treasure when they returned, but they did discover tobacco, and they started to grow it in plantations. Next they brought sugar plants from the Canary Islands, and soon sugar became the most important of all Caribbean crops.

By the middle of the 16th century Spanish treasure fleets, loaded with gold and silver from Peru and Mexico, were sailing through the Caribbean and across the Atlantic to Spain. The other seafaring nations were determined not to let Spain keep all this wealth for herself. So Dutch, Portuguese, French and English sea captains sailed to the Caribbean to fight the Spaniards for their treasure. For the next 200 years the Caribbean was a battleground for Europe's navies. Famous sea captains like Sir Francis Drake are the heroes of English history books, but in Spanish and Spanish American books they are shown as cruel and treacherous pirates, who killed, robbed and destroyed anything Spanish.

In the 17th and 18th centuries fierce naval wars were fought to capture and own the Caribbean islands, large and small. The Spanish kept Cuba, Hispaniola and Puerto Rico. The Dutch held on to Curaçoa, the French kept Martinique and Guadaloupe, and the British most of the rest.

The main crop on most islands was sugar. It was grown on

A Caribbean sugar mill in the days of slave labour

large plantations, which at once caused the planters problems. How were they going to cut the sugar canes, which were very thick and tough and between 3 and 8 metres tall? Like plantation owners in the Southern states of the USA, they bought African slaves from Portuguese, Dutch and British slave traders. The slave trade was very profitable to the British, since the plantations on the many British islands all needed workers. In those days, slavery was not considered wicked. Some African chiefs themselves sold strong, healthy men and women from their tribes to the European slave traders. For the long voyage the slaves were packed below decks like cattle, with hands and feet tied. If they complained they were beaten. Usually about a third of them died.

By the 18th century the British planters and their families were living comfortable lives in large, cool houses, looked after by well-trained black slaves. But many of the planters and their families spent most of their time in England, and left the plantation in the hands of managers, who usually had no kind feelings for the slaves. In some big islands like Jamaica, slaves who could escape ran and hid in the mountains, and formed bands armed with guns. These Maroons, as they were called, often defeated soldiers who were sent to capture them.

In 1833 the British government passed a law freeing all slaves. Many who had nowhere to go went on working on the plantations for a tiny wage. Others, who were lucky, got little plots of land and built huts and grew vegetables, or used the skills they had learned on the plantations and became carpenters, blacksmiths, mule drivers, cooks, children's nannies. There was a great deal of poverty, but not much bad feeling between blacks and whites. Since many blacks did not want to go back to work on the plantations, planters in Trinidad and Guyana had to bring in Indians from eastern India to take their place.

But West Indian society changed very slowly. Even though the slaves were freed, the whites continued to run the affairs of the islands, and most of the businesses. However, from the end of the 19th century onwards, the West Indians gradually ran their own affairs, and the education of the blacks improved.

By 1980, most of the British West Indian islands were independent nations, and most of these had decided to be members of the Commonwealth of Nations.

A   Vocabulary

1   What is a *landing*?
2   Give some examples of *treasure*?
3   What is the meaning of they *were wiped out*?
4   Find another way to say *loaded*.
5   What is the meaning of *cruel*?
6   What is a *problem*?
7   What is the meaning of *profitable*?
8   What does *well-trained* mean?

B   Questions

1 Why did Columbus call the natives 'Indians'?
2 What did the Spaniards hope to find on the islands?
3 What did the Spaniards do to the Arawaks?
4 What was the first crop the Spaniards grew on the islands?
5 What did the Spaniards think of Sir Francis Drake?
6 Who did the planters use to cut the sugar cane?
7 What did the planters do when they and their families went to England?
8 What did some of the slaves on Jamaican plantations do?

C   Grammar

What nouns do you get from the following adjectives?

important — treacherous — thick — profitable — wicked — comfortable — kind — lucky — independent — trained

and what adjectives from the following nouns?

cruelty — hero — tribe — freedom — law

D   Function

Disbelief

He'd never do a thing like that. — I can't believe that. — It's not possible. — It's very unlikely. — It's quite unlike him.

Use the phrases above to fill in the gaps.

Manager	Do you think he's run away?
You	. . .
Manager	Do you think it was he who shot the master?
You	. . . He admires him.
Manager	I'm sure he has joined the Maroons.

You   . . .
Manager   Why?
You   . . . He doesn't like fighting.
Manager   But do you think it was he who stole all those
                guns?
You   . . . He's not a thief.

22   The people and the outside world

There is no West Indian nation, or even a federation of
islands. Federation was tried in 1956, but did not work
satisfactorily because most of the islands had developed in
their own separate ways. Some are multi-racial. Trinidad has
almost as many East Indians as it has blacks. There are also
many people of mixed race and nationality, as well as
Chinese, Portuguese, French and British. Many Indians live
apart from the blacks and have kept their Hindu customs.
But every year all Trinidadians take part in the Carnival, and
anyone of any race can be chosen to play for the Trinidad
cricket team.

"mixed race and nationality"

The blacks in the Caribbean are prouder of being Jamaican, Barbadian, Trinidadian than of being West Indian. But they all share the same cheerful attitude to life, in spite of terrible poverty in towns like Kingston, Jamaica. The tropical or sub-tropical climate is a help. They can be out of doors most of the time, in their brightly coloured shirts and dresses, joking with each other, laughing a great deal, singing, dancing, and they do crazy things just because it amuses them. Drivers who meet a man walking along the white line in the middle of the road, arms outstretched as if he was a tightrope walker, are neither shocked nor surprised. The West Indians love noise and when they are excited they find it difficult to remain still—as anyone who sits behind them at a cricket match will know! They laugh and shout advice and insults at the players, beat on drums, and jump up and down.

West Indian barmen, waiters, or taxi drivers, do not treat customers differently because they are white, rich, or upper class. They believe in complete equality and a few American and British tourists are shocked at the way some West Indians treat them. Yet most blacks are very friendly and are thankful to see the growing number of tourists.

Ever since the early 1950s West Indians have been coming to Britain in the hope of getting a job and making a home. West Indian nurses were welcome in hospitals, and both hospital staff and patients had a high opinion of their skill and their gentleness. London Transport were also glad to have West Indian conductors and drivers. But many West Indians have been bitterly disappointed to find that they were not made welcome at all. Families of five have often had to live in one room and share a bathroom and toilet with three other families. They have missed the warmth, the blue skies and the cheerfulness of the Caribbean. But only a few can afford to go home. Many are unemployed, but they get the same welfare as every other British citizen. At home in the Caribbean, they would get very little help.

British influence in the Caribbean lies mostly in the past. Many of the British West Indian islands have a form of British parliamentary government, and a form of British law. Most of the islands belong to the Commonwealth of Nations. West

Indians also play cricket against other Commonwealth countries, and every four years there are the Commonwealth Games.

A political poster from Trinidad – the politicians are gobbling up the island

Cuban influence is largely political. Some West Indians admire Marxist Fidel Castro and admire the Cuban non-capitalist way of life. In 1976 the Jamaicans elected a left-wing government under Prime Minister Michael Manley, but in 1980, after fierce fighting in the streets of Kingston, a pro-American government was elected.

The Americans are determined to stop the spread of any form of Communism in the Caribbean, just as they are determined to stop the states of Central America from going Marxist. In 1979 the small but beautiful island of Grenada had a revolution and asked Cuba for arms and other help. Pictures of Fidel Castro were stuck on walls and trees all over the island. The new Marxist government called itself the People's Revolutionary Government, and started to build an airfield big enough to take the largest jets. In 1983 the Americans moved in, and after some fighting, took the island. They left when they felt the new government of Grenada was in control.

Most of the West Indian islands belong to the OAS (Organisation of American States). This helps them as regards trade. The USA has trade agreements with most of the islands, and Jamaica, for example, buys and sells more in the USA than anywhere else.

Although West Indians watch US television and enjoy it, their way of life has not been changed too much by American influence—except in the islands of the Bahamas, which lie so close to the USA.

A   Vocabulary

1   What is the meaning of *multi-racial*?
2   How would you say in other words *attitude to life*?
3   What do *outstretched arms* look like?
4   What is an *insult*?
5   What does a *barman* do?
6   What does *pro*-American mean?
7   What is a *jet*?

B   Questions

1   Why didn't the West Indies become a federation?
2   What is the unpleasant side of life in Kingston?
3   Why is there a white line down the middle of a road?
4   What jobs did the first West Indians get when they came to the UK?
5   Why was life so unpleasant for the West Indian immigrants?
6   What is the difference between the influence of Britain and the influence of Cuba in the West Indies?

7   What country helped the Grenada Revolution in 1979?
8   Why are the Bahamas more influenced by the USA than most other West Indian islands?

C   Grammar

Change the following sentences into the passive.

Example   The barman treated the customers badly.
The customers were treated badly by the barman.

1   The Jamaicans elected a left-wing government.
2   Television has changed their way of life.
3   They all share the same cheerful attitude to life.
4   London Transport gave jobs to the West Indians.
5   Their attitude has shocked and surprised me.
6   Boys stuck pictures of Fidel Castro on the walls.

D   Function

Saying thank you

Once again, thanks a lot. — That was kind of you. — That'd be terrific. — We're most grateful to you. — How kind of you. — That's very generous.

Fill in the gaps in the following dialogue.

West Indian	You can take my boat, if you like—£10 the whole day.
You	. . .
West Indian	No, not really
You	Well, . . .
West Indian	There's no need to be grateful. I'll come with you, if you like—no extra charge.
You	. . .
West Indian	I cleaned the boat yesterday.
You	See you 10 o'clock, then! . . .

23 West Indian islands—how they earn foreign currency

Gary Jackson looked back at his little group of tourists as they followed him past the patch of sugar cane. They were mostly Americans, British and Germans.

'Come with me, and I'll show you something,' he said, producing a murderous-looking knife. 'This is called a machete,' he explained.

They followed him to the edge of the little plantation. He stopped, and with three quick strokes cut three thick canes. 'That's how it used to be done before we had cane-cutting machines. Suck this piece of cane, and tell me what it tastes like!'

'It's exactly like brown sugar!' shouted a little American boy.

'Quite right, sonny!'

A Caribbean sugar mill

Gary's group climbed into the minibus, and soon they were driving up a narrow, twisting road, thickly shaded by a variety of trees. Gary stopped after a while and took the tourists into the forest.

'Most of these trees bear a fruit of some kind,' he said. 'See this big oval-shaped nut? Inside it are the cocoa beans which make chocolate. And over here is a coffee bush. It has white flowers, and the beans from which you make coffee are inside these hard little fruits here. See this little root under the ground?' He pulled it up. 'Smell it! That's what ginger comes from. Here's a nutmeg tree, and over there's a mango tree.

Higher up the hill, where the climate is not so hot, I'll show you some lemon and orange and grapefruit trees—but mixed plantations like this are no good for exports. The owner of this one sells his produce to the local markets, or to hotels.'

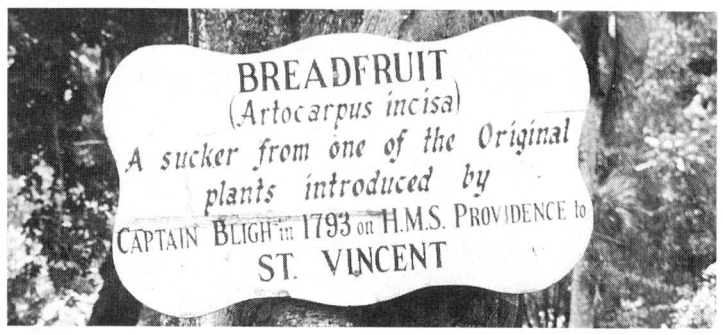

Gary's brother grows tomatoes, mangoes, coconuts, sweet potatoes and beans, which he sells to the hotels, but his main crop is bananas. He has about four acres of land divided into plots that he has to dig and harvest by hand. He also sells to hotels fish, which he catches from his small motor boat. Gary and his girl friend, who is a waitress in a hotel, sometimes go on fishing trips with him.

'Are there any big plantations on this island?' asked one of the tourists.

'Only of bananas and coconuts,' said Gary. 'Did you know bananas have the biggest leaves of any tree in the world?'

Many islands have coconut plantations. The hairy brown husk round the nut can be broken down into rough threads and made into mats or ropes. The white 'meat' of the coconut can be eaten, or used in the manufacture of sweets, or it can be turned into oil of all kinds for cooking, for making soap, for certain plastics, or for the brakes of automobiles. In large islands like Jamaica and Trinidad there is room for plantations of many kinds.

'Haven't you eaten bananas with a Jamaican label stuck on them?' Gary asked, 'or grapefruit from Trinidad, or bought a bottle of Jamaica rum back home? Rum is made from cane sugar, you know.'

> 'One of the nicest drinks in the West Indies is Rum Punch—rum mixed with a great variety of juices from local fruits.'
> F A Hoyos *Barbados Our Island Home*

Barbados is covered with sugar plantations. The centuries-old crop, sugar, is of great importance, even though the USA and Europe now get much of their sugar from the juicy root called the sugar beet. The main wealth of Trinidad and Tobago is mineral oil, but though oil is much the most important export, and Trinidad is better off than many of the islands, the Trinidadians do suffer from unemployment, which is the most worrying problem of the West Indian islands.

Tourism came to the help of the islands at just the right time, when many small industries were closing down. Gary's tourists included an American boy and his wealthy parents. They were staying in a cool, four-storey hotel with wide balconies. The parents spent much time at the well-stocked bar and under the palm trees on the terrace, sipping their iced drinks. They spent the rest of the time lying on the beach under umbrellas made of palm leaves. There were sailing boats of all sizes in the bay, and powerful motor-boats which took people on deep-sea fishing trips. Along the beach there was an even more expensive hotel, half of whose rooms consisted of suites (like flats).

Tourists come mostly from Britain and the USA, but more and more are also now coming from other Caribbean islands. Most islands earn a great many dollars and pounds from tourists. Tourism is an 'export' of blue skies, golden sands and warm blue-green sea, together with Caribbean song and dance, and friendly service.

Fishing for conch

A Vocabulary

1 What is the meaning of *patch* here?
2 Why is a machete a *murderous-looking* knife?
3 What kind of road is a *twisting* road?
4 What does *harvest* mean here?
5 What is a *husk*?
6 What do you sew on buttons with? The word is on the same page as 'husk'.
7 What does it mean when industries and firms *close down*?

B Questions

1 How did Gary cut the canes?
2 How are canes cut today on big plantations?
3 Do mangoes, nutmegs, cocoa beans, coffee beans, ginger grow on trees, bushes or under the ground?
4 What is unusual about the banana tree?
5 Why are coconuts such a valuable crop?
6 What is the difference between coconut oil and mineral oil from beneath the ground?

C   Grammar

Adjectives and nouns

Which adjectives fit which nouns?

    adjectives quick — oval-shaped — expensive — local —
sticky — iced — golden — worrying
nouns market — drink — label — strokes — problem —
sand — hotel — nuts

D   Function

Questions concerning time

    Please could you tell me what time it is?/What's the time,
please? — When does the plane to Tobago leave? — How
long will we have there? — What time should we get to the
airport? — Will there be time to drive round the island? —
How late will we be back?

Fill in the gaps in the dialogue using the phrases above.

Hotel receptionist	Can I help you, sir/madam?
Tourist	. . .
Receptionist	It's half past eight, sir/madam.
Tourist	. . .
Receptionist	At half past nine, sir/madam.
Tourist	. . .
Receptionist	You should be there by nine o'clock.
Tourist	. . .
Receptionist	You'll have six hours, sir/madam.
Tourist	. . .
Receptionist	You'll have plenty of time, sir/madam.
Tourist	. . .
Receptionist	You'll be back in time for dinner.

24 Cricket! Lovely cricket!

The West Indians learned cricket in the days of the British Commonwealth and Empire. They play football, too, but cricket is their national sport. In fact, it is a way of life which brings together people of all races and classes, the rich and the poor, and in no other Commonwealth country do women take such a passionate interest in the game. Most

Clive Lloyd, one of the great West Indian captains

Caribbean islands, or groups of islands, that were once British colonies, play cricket or watch it with patriotic excitement. During Test Matches, eyes are fixed on TV sets, ears to transistors, and youngsters climb coconut palms overlooking the cricket ground to get a free view. At an exciting moment in a game, all work may come to a stop. Sometimes, when spectators are angry with a player or an umpire, they throw bottles and cans onto the cricket field, and all the time they shout comments and advice to their own players: 'You do that again, Worrell, I send you back to the African jungle!'

The West Indians are natural cricketers. They don't need much coaching and they hit the ball at the right moment with the same ease as a good tennis player returning a difficult ball. They enjoy playing, and have developed qualities which since 1975 have made them the most powerful team in the world. Children play cricket on roads, on any open space, up against walls. If a boy is good, he may play for his island when he's 18, and perhaps for the West Indies when he's 20.

A sure way to make friends with a West Indian is to ask him about his local heroes. He'll tell you why they're great, using a good deal of technical language. In islands like Jamaica, where unemployment is high and homes can be over-crowded and squalid, success in cricket is a sure way up the ladder from poverty. Some of the greatest West Indian cricketers have been knighted by the Queen (Worrell became 'Sir Frank Worrell'). Being top nation in Common-wealth cricket has given West Indians a great pride, and has helped towards a certain unity among the independent islands. They are respected, admired throughout the Commonwealth—and feared, for they have the fastest bowlers in the world. Only in the Bahamas is cricket not the national game. There baseball and American football are played, thanks to the influence of the USA. The islands that were never British colonies do not play cricket.

So many black West Indians are fine athletes. At the Commonwealth Games, the 100 metre relay teams of Jamaica and Trinidad have won gold medals. The children and grandchildren of West Indian immigrants in Britain have raised British hopes in both track and field events. Several are football (soccer) and rugby league stars, and some have played cricket for England.

The West Indians are a naturally musical people. It was the Trinidadians who invented the steel band, one of the most extraordinary musical inventions ever made. Young Trinidadians made the discovery when they started banging on empty oil drums, left behind by the American troops who were in Trinidad during World War 2. They found that each drum when hit made a different noise, so they started tuning them until every note, bass and treble, could be 'drummed'. Years later a Trinidadian steel band was invited to Vienna, where they played Mozart to a surprised and enthusiastic audience.

The rhythmical beating of drums goes way back to their ancestors in Africa. Africans today still beat drums on special occasions. But in the West Indies steel drums can also accompany calypsos, a form of Caribbean folk song which was first sung in Trinidad. Calypsos have a strong, simple rhythm. The words are sometimes written down, but the best calypsos are invented by the singer as he goes along, and they have as their subject matter unpopular politicians, exciting events, cricket victories (*Cricket! Lovely cricket!*). Competitions are held during Trinidad's Carnival festivities and the singer who gets the most votes is given the title 'King' or 'Queen' Calypsonian. American musicians have also had a strong influence on the island ever since US troops were there in the war. Trinidadians visit Louisiana and bring back the latest music from America.

Carnival was brought to Trinidad by the French. It is the main event in the Trinidadian calendar, starting after Christmas and reaching its most exciting moments during the last two days before Ash Wednesday. Then all work stops and crowds move through the streets, dancing and singing and wearing all kinds of different costumes. There are groups dressed as policemen or characters from the Bible, animals, birds, insects. Some walk on tall stilts (long sticks), swaying above the crowd.

Carnival has come to England, to Notting Hill in London, where there are many West Indian immigrants. It has become popular with the whole neighbourhood. Everyone joins in, even the police.

A Carnival dancer dressed as an African witchdoctor

A   Vocabulary

1   What does *national sport* mean?
2   What is a *youngster*?
3   What does a *spectator* do?
4   What does *squalid* mean?
5   In what way is an *audience* different from spectators?
6   What do you find on a *calendar*?
7   What do you do with a *costume*?

B   Questions

1   People in the West Indies don't only love playing cricket,
     they also ...
2   What is meant by a 'natural cricketer'?
3   Which cricket team is the most powerful at the moment,
     the English or the West Indian team?
4   Name one thing that cricket has done for the West Indies.
5   Name two islands that do not play cricket. Why don't
     they play?
6   How did the Trinidadians discover that metal drums
     could be used as musical instruments?
7   How long does Carnival last in Trinidad?

C   Grammar

Turn the sentences into the negative, using short forms.

Example   He had a passionate nature.
           He *didn't have* a passionate nature.

The umpire stopped the game. — You find cold days in the
jungle. — He's a hero. — It's a technical matter. — This music
has got rhythm. — There were festivities. — He accompanied
the tourists. — The tree is swaying.
(NB Two sentences without an article, *a* or *the*, need the
addition of *any* before the noun.)

D   Function

Wanting to buy something

How much is it? — Right, I'll take it. — It's too much. — Have
you got one that's less expensive? — I want that steel
drum. — Yes, I do/Yes, I want to buy it. — Please send it to
my hotel.

Boy/girl friend	*What do you want?*
You	. . .
Friend	Do you really want to buy it?
You	. . .
Friend	You'd better ask how much it is first.
You	OK. Excuse me, . . .
Shop assistant	It's £30.
You	I'm afraid . . .
Shop assistant	You can have this one for £20.
You	Thank you very much. . . .
Shop assistant	Will you take it with you?
You	No. . . .

25   How the Caribbean islanders speak

The Caribs (on the mainland) gave the Spaniards a number of words which are in everyday use in Spain and have become part of the English language: *huracán* (hurricane), *maiz* (maize), *tabaco* (tobacco). One of the names the Caribs were called, according to Christopher Columbus, was *Canibales*. As the Spaniards discovered that they ate their male captives, they used the word for humans who eat human flesh—in English, *cannibals*. The best known Arawak word, Jamaica (*xaymaca*) is said to mean 'Land of Springs'.

In the 16th and 17th centuries, Spanish was the most common European language spoken in the Caribbean, and Spanish still remains the language of Cuba, Hispaniola (Haiti and the Dominican Republic) and the American island, Puerto Rico. French is spoken in Martinique and Guadaloupe and Dutch in Curaçoa. But in most of the other islands, English is the official language.

The black slaves who worked on the sugar plantations came mostly from West Africa, where many different languages were spoken, and where some of the tribes were bitter enemies. So there must have been many cases where slaves could not or would not explain to newcomers what their masters expected of them. For a hundred years no attempt was made to teach slaves English, except for the house slaves. Gradually there grew up a number of Caribbean or 'Creole' languages, in which the slaves were able to talk to one another. All these Creole languages had an African 'sing-song' sound and a rich mixture of English words strung together by a syntax, or grammar, very different from that of standard English.

Most British West Indian islands have two languages, standard English and Creole. St Lucia's Creole is based on French, since the island belonged to France from the 17th century until 1814. Tourists do not understand a word of it, sometimes not even French tourists. Trinidad – which is the Spanish for 'Trinity' – was a Spanish colony for 300 years. Then in 1797 it became British. The Spaniards neglected the island and encouraged French planters to settle there. So it was the French rather than the Spanish who influenced the Trinidad language, though an English Creole language grew up later.

The Indians who came to work in the plantations of Trinidad and British Guyana between 1844 and 1917 brought their customs, their religion and their language with them. Most of them were Hindus and spoke Hindi, while the Muslims spoke Urdu. They usually spoke their own language among themselves, but also learned English, or developed a dialect of their own.

Perhaps the best place to study a Creole language is Jamaica. The British captured the island in 1655 and it remained British until it became independent in 1962. There are two main languages spoken in Jamaica: standard Jamaican English and what is known as 'Jamaica Talk', which is a real Creole language, not just English spoken badly. Some words in its vocabulary are made up of two or more words run together: *dweet* (do it), *gwaan* (go on), Susie *go-a-town* hat (the hat Susie wears for going to town). Even educated English people sometimes run several words together when they are talking with one another: 'My wife goes to the West

Indies every year.' 'Djemaker?'[1] ('Do you make her?'—but it sounds like 'Jamaica') 'No, she goes of her own accord.'

Speakers of Jamaica Talk do not use plurals. A man wears 'a trousers'. A woman cuts cloth with 'a scissors'. 'Gary and Viv *was* good frien'.' At the beginning of a word, *d* takes the place of *th*. '*De* girl say she don't know *dat* man.'[1] Verb endings and tenses are not important in Jamaica Talk. 'A *ben* go las' Monday ...'[2], 'De baby come boan Tuesday.'[3], 'De postman don't come yet.'[4], 'Him don't do nuttn'.' could mean either, 'He *doesn't* do anything.' or 'He *hasn't done* anything.' or 'He *hadn't done* anything.' It will be clear from the pronunciation, and from the rest of the conversation, which of these it is. Pronouns, too, are not used in the standard English way: 'Dat girl wear *she* hat.', '*She* family no let *she* in house.' (her).

Sometimes Jamaica Talk gives a word a completely different meaning: 'Him kick my daughter. I'se very *ignorant*.' Here *ignorant* means *indignant*. Spoken in its pure form, only someone from Jamaica would understand it, but usually quite a lot of standard Jamaican English is mixed in with it. In fact, Jamaicans quite often speak a mixture of Jamaica Talk and standard English, while keeping the sing-song sound and the Creole pronunciation of many of the words. 'I t'ink so, sah!' would not be difficult for anyone to understand. More and more Jamaicans are speaking standard English, because it is important for the tourist trade.

Many of the British who live in the Caribbean speak a form of Jamaica Talk.

A   Vocabulary

1   What is a *hurricane*?
2   What is an *official language*?
3   How do you *neglect* people?
4   Give the meaning of: *she goes of her own accord*.
5   What is the English meaning of *ignorant*?
6   What does *indignant* mean?
7   Translate into standard English: *Dat girl wear she hat* and *She family no let she in house*.

1   The girl says she doesn't know that man.
2   I went last Monday ...
3   The baby was born on Tuesday.
4   The postman hasn't come yet.

B   Questions

1   What language did most Europeans speak in the Caribbean during the 16th century?
2   What countries make up Hispaniola?
3   Why was it difficult for the early slaves to know what their masters expected of them?
4   What languages did the Indians speak when they settled in Trinidad?
5   What is the Creole language of Jamaica often called?
6   What is important for the tourist trade in the West Indies?

C   Grammar

Tenses

Turn the paragraph beginning 'The black slaves . . .' into the present tense. Once or twice the present perfect, the future or future perfect will be required.

D   Function

Questions at a West Indian tourist office

Fill in the dialogue with questions which suit the phrases in brackets.

You	. . . (next plane Heathrow)
Girl in tourist office	There's a plane at 10.30 in the morning.
You	. . . (change)
Girl	Yes, in Barbados.
You	. . . (how long)
Girl	About eight hours.
You	. . . (reserve)
Girl	Yes. First Class or Tourist?
You	. . . (bus to airport)
Girl	Yes, it will pick you up at the hotel at 9 o'clock.

Africa

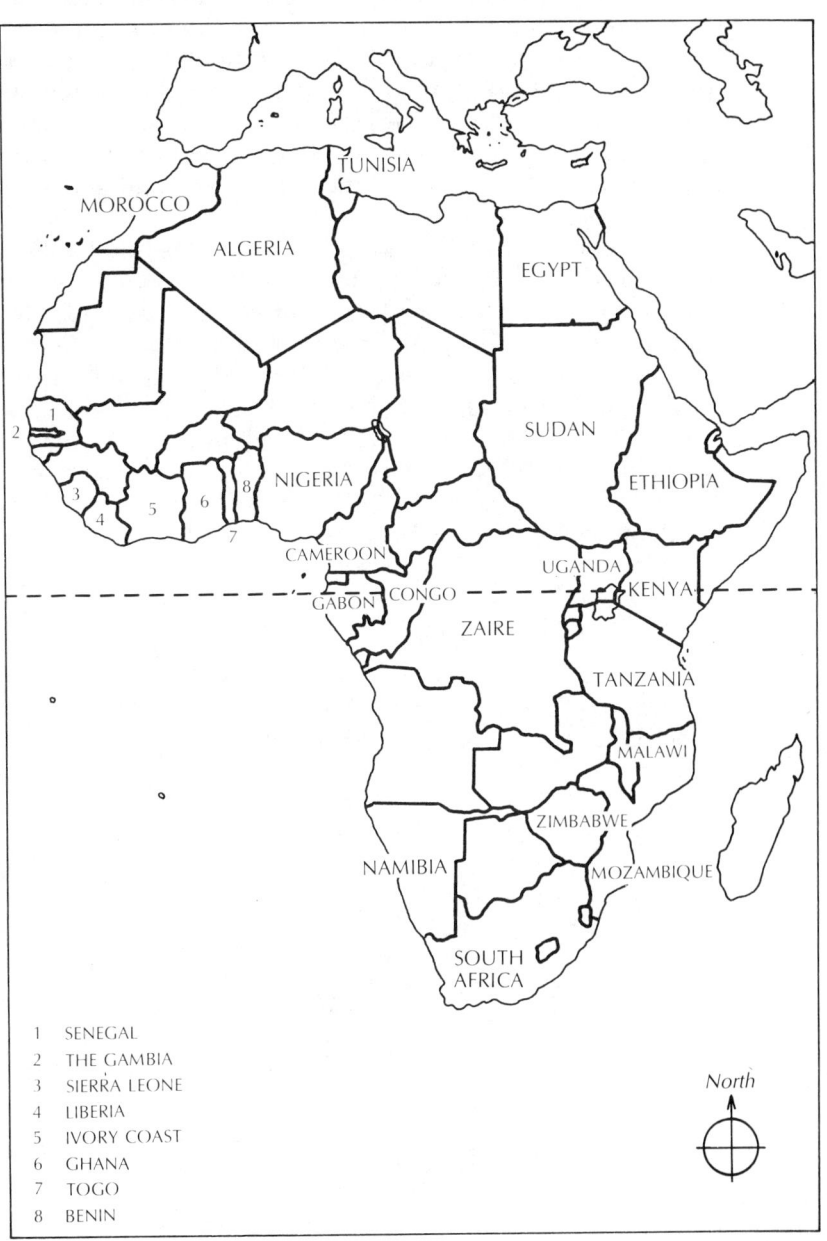

1 SENEGAL
2 THE GAMBIA
3 SIERRA LEONE
4 LIBERIA
5 IVORY COAST
6 GHANA
7 TOGO
8 BENIN

26 From colony to freedom— North and West Africa

Every independent country in Africa has with one exception been the colony of a European nation. The exception is Liberia, the oldest African republic, founded in 1882 as a place where escaped American slaves could live in safety. Ethiopia, taken by the Italians under Mussolini in 1936, was a colony for only five years, for the British defeated the Italian army in 1941, during the Second World War, and gave the country back its freedom.

The Europeans wanted colonies for several reasons. Prestige was one reason—people felt proud that their country owned a slice of Africa. A more important reason was trade. In Africa there are many different kinds of valuable things. There are coconuts and cocoa, all kinds of fruits and spices, timber (mahogany and ebony), and ivory. There are also many different kinds of minerals. A colony was valuable to an industrial country if it could supply raw materials like cotton or sisal (for making string and rope), or minerals like iron ore, copper or gold. For very low wages 'native' workers dug out the minerals and grew the crops, which were shipped to British factories. Some of the manufactured goods from these raw materials were sold back to the colonies, which were always good markets.

Look at the map and you will see which European
countries had colonies. Germany took Togoland (now Togo)
in 1884 and lost it to Britain after World War 1. Britain had the
largest and richest share, while France owned most of
northern Africa including the Sahara Desert. France and
Britain were as always great rivals.

France meant to have a solid block of Africa from the
Atlantic to the Red Sea. The British wished to have a solid
strip of territory from the Nile delta in Egypt to the Cape in
South Africa. Both countries sent expeditions to claim
southern Sudan. The French, having crossed the Sahara from
Gabon, reached the Upper Nile at Fashoda and raised the
French flag. The British arrived eight days later. There was no
battle, but the British took the Sudan, through an agreement
with the French Government. In 1956 the Sudan became an
independent republic.

Nigeria was first explored by the Royal Niger Company,
which had its own army. The soldiers called the Africans
'savages' and killed them by the hundred. It made no
difference that the 'savages' were defending their own
country. What mattered was that they were stopping the
Company in its search for wealth. When Nigeria became an
official colony in 1888 the people were much better treated,
and some were educated and brought into the government
of the colony.

In all European countries with African colonies, there
were people who cared about the well-being of the Africans.
But they did not have nearly such a strong influence as the
traders or the soldiers who were not worried if the boundaries
of the colonies they formed cut through the middle of
different African peoples. It did not matter to them if a large
colony like Nigeria had inside its borders at least three
important African peoples. The Hausas and Fulanis in the dry
semi-desert of the north, though black, have Arab blood in
them and are Muslims, and their whole way of life is much
closer to the Hausas and Fulanis of Niger, Mali and Sierra
Leone than to the Ibos and Yorubas of Southern Nigeria. The
River Niger and its great tributary, the Benue, form natural
frontiers for the Hausas, Yorubas and the Ibos. After Nigeria

British soldiers in the Sudan

got its independence in 1960 the Ibos wished to found an independent nation called Biafra. There was a long and bitter civil war. When it was over, the Nigerians showed the world the meaning of forgiving and forgetting. After the Civil War there was a military government. In the last twenty years the government has changed often, and there have been military as well as civilian governments. Nigeria's chief problem, and it is one of Ghana's chief problems too, is narrowing the gap between the tiny minority of very rich and the great majority of poor, many of whom can neither read nor write. Both countries, especially Nigeria, have natural wealth, but they don't always make the most of it. Competition for markets is so strong these days.

Sierra Leone and The Gambia make up the quartet of ex-British colonies in West Africa. The Gambia is a perfect example of a country with unsuitable frontiers. It stretches for about 250 miles on either side of the Gambia river and it is nowhere more than 30 miles wide. It has a population of 600,000 and is surrounded on all sides by French-speaking Senegal whose people are no different from them, either in race or language. At independence they were given the chance of becoming part of Senegal, but they chose to stay on their own. They are now better off than Senegal.

A   Vocabulary

1   'George couldn't speak Yoruba well, but everyone else could.' Rewrite the sentence, using the word *exception*.
2   When the enemy has lost the battle, you say, . . . (defeat) . . .
3   What does *prestige* mean?
4   What is the difference in shape between a *block* and a *strip*?
5   Three words have been used for the edge of a country. What are they?
6   What does it mean when you *forgive* someone?

B   Questions

1   There is something unusual about Liberia. What is it?
2   Ethiopia was occupied by the Italians in 1936. When did it get back its independence, and who freed it?
3   What is the difference between mahogany and cocoa, and what do they have in common?
4   What is the meaning of 'to ship' something?
5   What happened to the Sudan after the Fashoda incident?
6   Many soldiers of the Royal Niger Company treated the Africans with cruelty. What was their excuse?
7   Why does Nigeria have unsatisfactory borders?
8   What was the cause of the Nigerian Civil War?
9   Why was it so surprising that the Gambia decided not to join up with Senegal after independence?

C   Grammar

Which tense?

Answer the questions with the correct form of tense, using pronouns when possible, and short forms where suitable.
Example   Why was Mrs Tokoto so worried?
            (because — son — hunt — man-eating lion)
            Because her son was hunting a man-eating lion.

1   What happened to Mr Nwanze? (eat — crocodile)
2   Why are you going up the Niger? (want — see — hippopotamus)
3   What would you do if you met a rhino? (run fast)
4   Why didn't Mr Omo leave Sierra Leone? (because — police — take — passport)
5   What are you going to do tomorrow? (go — Lagos)
6   Why are you so miserable? (because boy/girlfriend — go back — England) (Two answers are possible here. Give both)

D   Function

Questions and answers at an interview

You are applying for a teaching job in an African school.

Interviewer	Your name in full, please.
You	...
Interviewer	Where do you live?
You	...
Interviewer	Have you ever been to a Third World country before?
You	...
Interviewer	Do you speak any African languages?
You	...

Now continue the interview. What other facts might the interviewer want to know about you?

27   Freedom for some— in East, Central and Southern Africa

Long ago, in the 13th century, Arab traders settled along the East African coast. They intermarried with African farmers and fishermen, and out of this union grew a new society.

When Vasco de Gama reached East Africa from Portugal in 1498, he was surprised to find that the people were civilised, living in beautiful houses surrounded by flowering gardens. But other Portuguese who came after him were only interested in trade, in the spices and ivory they found. As for the people, Portuguese soldiers attacked and destroyed Mombasa, killing every man, woman and child.

Then in the last twenty years of the 19th century the great rush for colonies began. The British had already occupied the island of Zanzibar. They now seized Kenya and Uganda. The Germans took Tanganyika (Tanzania), the Belgians took the Congo (Zaire), the Portuguese held on to Mozambique.

Rhodesia, in central Africa, was named after Cecil Rhodes, a British diamond millionaire. Seeing how good the land was for farming, he paid 200 settlers to go and claim the territory for Britain. Rhodesia was divided into two colonies, Southern Rhodesia (Zimbabwe), colonised by white settlers, and Northern Rhodesia (Zambia). 'The British are the first race in the world,' wrote Rhodes, 'and the more of it we inhabit, the better for the human race.' At that time there were quite a lot of British people who felt like him. Nyasaland (Malawi) and Bechuanaland (Botswana) were also added to the British Empire.

The Dutch colonised the Cape (the southern tip of Africa) in the 17th century. But after the British had seized their colony in 1806 they made their famous trek* into the unknown north, where they founded two republics, the Transvaal and the Orange Free State. A little later the British in Cape Colony founded Natal. A fight between the British and the Dutch (now called 'Boers') had to come, for the British were determined to unite the whole of southern

The Great Trek

trek journey

Africa under their rule. The Boers were equally determined to hold on to their independence. In 1899 the British and the Dutch in Southern Africa went to war. The war (known as the Boer War) lasted nearly three years, and the British only won after terrible losses, and after 20,000 Boer women and children had died of neglect in British concentration camps.

After the war the British Government united the British and the Boers (now called 'Afrikaners') in the Union of South Africa, which in 1919 became a self-governing Dominion. Since the Afrikaners had a majority of 6 to 4 over the English-speaking South Africans, they took control of the government and have kept it ever since. But the British government neglected to protect the 20,000,000 non-whites, who were given no power at all.

In 1948 the South African government passed the Apartheid Laws, which meant that non-whites were forced to live separate lives in terrible conditions, and to work for the whites in unskilled jobs for very low wages. The average earnings of white South Africans today is about 13 times higher than the average earnings of black South Africans, and the blacks are still not citizens of South Africa. Instead they have been given 'homelands' inside the Union, where they can run their own affairs, work for themselves, etc. But the homelands are miserable places, and the people are not really free. Most of them still have to earn their living by working in South African cities, and are forced to live in slumlike townships. They will not be satisfied now until they get full South African citizenship, 'one man, one vote'. Their leaders are becoming stronger and are ready to go to prison for their beliefs. Hundreds of Africans have been killed in battles with the police. Whites have died too.

After World War 1 the UK took Tanganyika (now Tanzania) from Germany, and German South West Africa (Namibia) went to South Africa. After World War 2 all British colonies in Africa gradually got their freedom, but between 1952–56 the Kikuyu people of Kenya fought for their independence in what is called the Mau Mau uprising. They were defeated. But the British made Jomo Kenyatta the first Prime Minister of independent Kenya, even though they had imprisoned him, believing him to be the leader of Mau Mau in 1963. Kenyatta showed no bitterness towards the British, but invited them to stay on. Before independence 41,000 white Kenyans ruled over 11,000,000 Africans. There are still about 40,000 whites in Kenya today.

At the same time in Southern Rhodesia, 251,000 whites ruled over 5,300,000 Africans. The whites wanted complete independence from Britain. This was refused, because the whites offered the blacks so little share in the government. The white Rhodesians resisted the British Government and voted themselves independent. Britain and many other countries stopped trading with Rhodesia, while the whites also had to fight African freedom fighters. White Rhodesians at last had to give in and accept 'one man, one vote'—which meant that when Rhodesia became independent and held its first elections, there was a huge black majority. In 1981 Robert Mugabe became the first black Prime Minister of Zimbabwe.

A   Vocabulary

1 Explain *intermarry.*
2 What does to *occupy* a town mean?
3 Find another word for *territory.*
4 What is a *concentration camp*?
5 What do you think is meant by *terrible conditions*?
6 What is your idea of a *slumlike township*?
7 What does the ordinary citizen do in an *election*?

B   Questions

1 What did the Portuguese do to the people of Mombasa?
2 How did Rhodes become a millionaire?
3 What did Rhodes think about the British?
4 What did the Boers call their two independent territories?
5 The British were generous in one way when they united South Africa, but what did they neglect to do at the same time?

6   What sort of complaints do the Africans have about their treatment by the whites?
7   Would you say that Kenyatta was generous to the white Kenyans? If so, why?

C   Grammar

The negative

Write a letter home about a not very successful holiday in East Africa, using as many of these words and phrases as possible.

not — n't — never — no one/nobody — nowhere — nothing — none — neither ... nor — uncomfortable — awful/such an awful — terrible — rude — nasty — unsuccessful — unfortunate

D   Function

How do I get there?

You are in Kenyatta Avenue, Nairobi, and want to get to the railway station. Look at the map and then, using some of the phrases below, make up two dialogues between yourself and a passer-by who tells you which way to go: 1) on foot 2) by car. Use any other phrases you can think of and make the instructions as full as possible.

Please can you tell me the way? — Is it far/a long walk? — Do I pass the Hilton? — The car's parked in Kimathi Street. — Did you say right or left? — Will it take long? — Sorry to trouble you.

... first, second, third turning on the left/right — You can't miss it. — round the roundabout — across the road — straight ahead — on the other side of — at the crossroads — not far/quite far — opposite/facing you — It's been a pleasure.

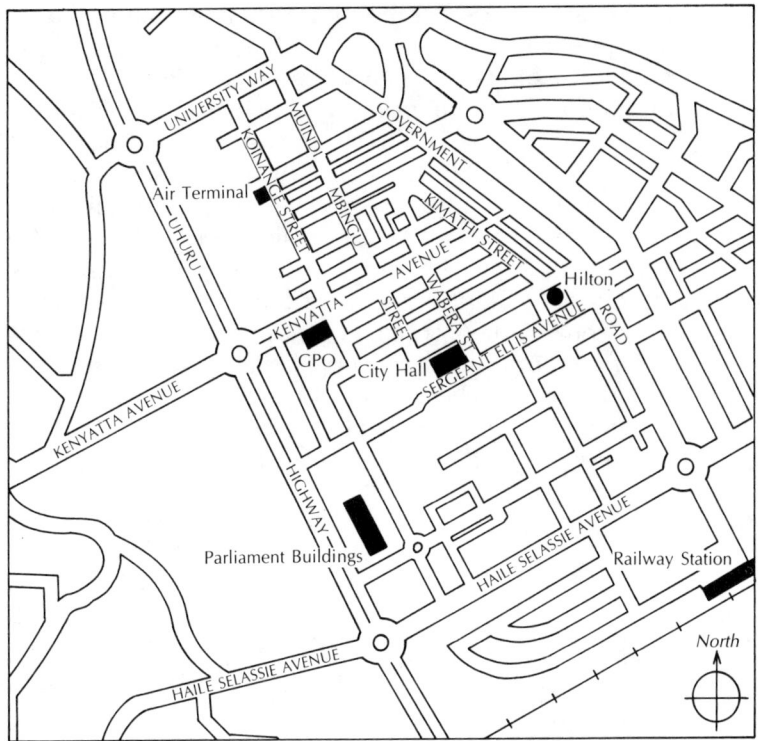

28 Oil and cocoa, tea and coffee

There are strong contrasts between East Africa and West Africa. If you look at the map of Africa, you will see that the equator crosses the continent from Kenya on the Indian Ocean to Gabon on the Atlantic. Only 5° north of Gabon lies the most thickly populated state in Africa, Nigeria. Nigeria and Kenya are very different, though both are on, or close to, the equator.

Nigeria is a truly tropical country. In the southeast it is hot and steamy during the whole year, and the temperature hovers around 35° for month after month, but in the north, on the edge of the Sahara, it is hot and dry and there are more dust storms than rain. There are millions and millions of mosquitoes in the mangrove swamps of the Niger's huge delta, and malaria is still a common disease. Today malaria can be controlled by drugs, but the hospitals and doctors do not have enough drugs to deal with it. In colonial times few Europeans settled with their families in Nigeria. It was not a land to settle in. The men who came were prospectors, or traders, or soldiers. In the early days these people knew that they would certainly catch malaria or some other fatal fever.

For centuries millions of Africans have suffered from malaria, too. Malaria rarely kills, but once someone has caught it, it never completely goes away. Every now and then it returns, weakening the body and the will to work.

Lagos, Nigeria

Nigeria has enough raw materials of all kinds to be one of the richest countries in Africa. Oil was not discovered until 1950, but now, among the network of channels in the Niger Delta, rise the steel pyramids of Nigeria's 'oil plantations'.

Cities like Lagos have skyscrapers and traffic jams; at the same time 70% of Nigerians live away from the cities in villages, raising cattle, growing maize, millet, yams, cassava. Though poor compared with most Europeans, Nigerian farmers and their families do get enough to eat. In the meantime, Nigerian trade with the outside world is growing. Apart from her oil exports, Nigeria is one of the leading exporters of cocoa. She also exports vast quantities of peanuts, as well as rubber and palm seeds (from which soap is made). The UK has remained Nigeria's main trading partner.

'The cocoa tree is a native of the Amazon region of South America and was brought to West Africa about 100 years ago. The climate and soils of western Nigeria are ideal for growing it. Cocoa trees need plenty of shade and are grown under taller trees.'

Ghana on the West coast of Africa was once a British colony—called the Gold Coast because it was a major gold producer. Ghana still ranks fifth as an exporter of gold, after South Africa, the USSR, Canada and the USA. But much the most valuable of Ghana's exports is cocoa. She is way ahead of all other cocoa-producing countries, and produces nearly twice as much cocoa a year as Nigeria.

If you enter Kenya through Uganda, you will find that the land soon begins to rise. Kenya's rolling uplands climb to over 2500 m, and away to the south the needle-sharp peaks of Mount Kenya rise to 5200m. As you move further inland, you may well come across a Kikuyu farmer on horseback, riding round his coffee plantation. You are only a few miles from the equator, but the air is fresh and cool in this highland region, and when the farmer invites you to his attractive farmhouse and you sit outside with him in the warm sunshine, he will tell you that his years spent at college in Nairobi have helped him to grow good crops.

'My son is a ranger in one of the wild game reserves. His main job is to protect elephants from ivory poachers*.'

poachers thieves

'What about the white farmers? Is there bad feeling between you?'

'No. We each lead our own lives. Many of the whites have Kenyan passports. We are not working against each other. Trade is good in Kenya.'

'Do many foreign tourists visit your game parks?'

'More and more. Tourism is already an important part of our national income. Tourists also go to Mombasa. It's an interesting old town and there are some lovely beaches.'

'What are your main crops?'

'Tea, coffee, different grains, sisal—they are grown mostly in what used to be called the White Highlands, where the Englishmen had their farms. There are still some whites there. Kenyatta bought out the rest at a fair price. He believed in capitalism, but he also helped the small farmers. He grouped them together in co-operatives so that they could share work and profits.'

A   Vocabulary

1   Give a simple example of a *contrast*.
2   Describe a *swamp*.
3   What happens when a disease is *fatal*?
4   What is a *delta*?
5   What is a *traffic jam*?
6   What is meant by *rolling uplands*?
7   Name a few *raw materials*.
8   What is a *major* producer?

B   Questions

1   What are the differences between Northern and Southern Nigeria?
2   Why did so few whites take their families to live with them in West Africa?
3   It has been said that malaria has been the most serious obstacle to progress in West Africa. Give some reasons why this might be so.

4   Nigeria is fairly near the equator. The equator passes right through Kenya. Yet is is pleasanter to live in the Kenyan uplands than in the delta of the Niger. Why?
5   Why are there wild game reserves in so many African countries, and what place does the ranger have in them?

C   Grammar

1   There are 25 uncountable nouns in this unit—nouns which take a singular verb and pronoun, and are not often used with 'a', 'an', 'one', 'two', etc.
2   There are 2 nouns in this unit which only take a plural verb and plural pronouns – eg *The police are at the football match. They . . .*

See how many of each kind you can find, and make up short sentences with them, using as many words in one sentence as you like.

Example Maize grows well in the sunshine.

Some of these nouns can be used in the plural, but then their meaning is different, eg *land, lands*.

D   Function

Reluctance

Must I? — Do I really have to? — Why do I have to? — I'm too tired. — Because I don't like/enjoy game parks at all. — All right, if I must, but I don't see why I should. — No, golf is not nearly so tiring.

Using the phrases above, make up a dialogue between a husband and wife. The wife wants to go to a game park. The husband would rather play golf. Think of something which finally makes the husband agree.

Wife   I'd love you to drive me to a game park today.
Husband . . .

29 Sport in Africa

There is a great future for African athletes, who have already made their mark in the world records books. Africa's greatest runners have so far come from the west or north west of the continent. John Akii-Bua is an exception. He is a Ugandan, and in the Munich Olympic Games broke the 400 m hurdles record. Jipcho Keino of Kenya broke the 3000 m steeplechase record at the Helsinki Games in 1974, and Abebe Bikila of Ethiopia won the marathon twice running, in 1960 and 1964, while Mamo Wolde, another Ethiopian, won in 1968. These and other athletes from Kenya, Ethiopia and Tunisia also won gold medals for other distances between 1960 and 1980. In 1972 Kenya won the gold medal for the 4 × 400 m relay, which is, perhaps the most remarkable win of all.

Few people know much about African football, yet the Africans are enthusiastic players and draw enthusiastic crowds.

Ifeanyi Onyedika of Nigeria

African football is organised very much like European football. Teams have names like *Enugu Rangers* and *Shooting Stars*. Each country has leagues and championships, and the winner of the League Championship competes for the African Champion Club Cup. The Francophone countries have so far done much better than the Anglophone countries. Clubs from the Cameroun (4 wins), Guinea (3), Zaire (3), Algeria, Ivory Coast, Congo, Egypt have all won the Cup. As in Europe there is also a Cup Winner's Cup, which Cameroun and Nigeria have each won twice and Guinea has won once.

In sport as in most other things the Bantu, the black people of South Africa, cannot organise events as they would like to. Football is their favourite game, but though they can arrange matches and have football grounds of their own, they cannot play international or club matches before their own people in fine modern stands, as most independent African peoples can. They have to play on grounds chosen for them by white officials. So most countries in the world have boycotted South African sport and will continue to do so until whites and non-whites play together in complete equality. South Africa has been banned from the Olympic Games, the Davis Cup (tennis), and all other international sports meetings. This is a serious blow to the white South Africans, since sport – and above all, victory in sport – means more to them than to almost any other people.

Rugby is the white South African national game. The South Africans have an even greater passion for rugby than the New Zealanders, and the two of them are generally regarded as having the best teams in the world. So it was a bitter blow when the New Zealanders cancelled their tour in 1967. The reason was, the South African Prime Minister refused to accept the Maoris who had been picked for the All Black side. But the South African public made such an outcry that the Prime Minister gave way. The All Blacks of 1970 were the first multi-racial team ever to visit South Africa. At the end of the seventies the South African Government allowed multi-racial sport. It made little difference to the Bantu and it made no impression at all on the governments of the outside world. But the South Africans encouraged unofficial tours by offering big money rewards. Some foreign cricketers could not resist the temptation, in spite of warnings that they would be punished. A powerful team of West Indians accepted, and were banned by their governments from ever playing for the West Indies or their islands again. Unofficial teams also came from Sri Lanka, Australia and England. They too were punished, though not so severely.

Music and dancing

Every African country, every tribe, has its own special dances. Some dance troupes have toured Europe and the USA, and they are a tremendous success, for top African dancers are both graceful and lively. They still dance tribal dances which are centuries old, and which tell stories or suggest birth or death or love. The male dancers perform

African trumpets and drums

fierce and tremendously energetic war dances which used to excite African warriors before they went into battle.

Singing once played a very important part in African life, and still does in South Africa. Messengers 'sing' secret warnings and orders from their leaders which only the Bantu can understand. The Kikuyu passed on messages in this way during the Mau Mau uprising. Singing among Africans today helps keep tribes united and builds up patriotism.

African music has very little melody but a great deal of rhythm and the human voice and drums are the most common instruments. Many African societies are now influenced by black American music, and on the East coast by Indian music, too.

A   Vocabulary

1   How would you say in simple English *have already made their mark in . . .* ?
2   Explain. He won *twice running.*
3   How do you feel when you're *enthusiastic*?
4   What happens when you are *banned*?
5   How would you explain the word *passion* as used on page 153, line 27?
6   What do you do when you *cancel* something?
7   Name something, an animal for example, which people consider *graceful.*

B   Questions

1   Do you consider that Kenya's 'gold' in the 4 × 400 m relay was remarkable? If so, why?
2   Are you enthusiastic about football? What is your favourite sport?
3   Why are the Bantu in South Africa less fortunate in sport than most other Africans?
4   What do many white South Africans love most about sports?

5   For what political purpose is singing sometimes used in South Africa today?

C   Grammar

Use the form 'in order to' in completing the following sentences. Once or twice you may feel you can use 'to' by itself.

Example   (win) his gold medal, Jipcho Keino had to train hard.
In order to win his gold medal, Jipcho Keino had to train hard.

1   He watched the Shooting Stars team (learn about football).
2   (help fight) Apartheid, the Commonwealth has boycotted South African sport.
3   You don't have to fight (win)!
4   Must you have long legs (run fast)?
5   The South African government introduced multi-racial sport (encourage) other countries to visit South Africa.

D   Function

Praising someone (who has won an important race)

Congratulations! — It was a great victory. — Oh, it certainly wasn't luck! — You were great. — Of course it wasn't your fault that he fell over. — You were terrific. — No, don't argue! — We all think you're the greatest runner the college has ever had. — Dipo? Good Heavens, no! He was like an old elephant compared to you.

Make up a dialogue between Yemi and his friend Wole, a very modest runner who has won a good race, but feels he was lucky. He bumped into the leading runner by mistake and knocked him out of the race. He doesn't feel his friend's admiration is deserved.

30 A multitude of languages

There are known to be at least a thousand completely different languages in Africa. There are 200 in Nigeria alone.

English has remained the official language in most countries which were once British colonies, because except for Swahili, spoken in East Africa, most African languages are local, or tribal. Although in Nigeria, for example, country people can usually speak two or more local languages, if they wish to do business in Lagos or any of the other big cities, they have to speak English—except in the north, where nearly everybody speaks Hausa. In fact, in business and politics and universities, English is the official language.

Africans in ex-British colonies who go to live in the growing cities must learn English if they want to get on, and more and more country people are moving to the cities to find work. College students listen to lectures delivered in English by African as well as British lecturers, and in the city bookshops there is a wide variety of books and journals published in English as well as in Swahili and Hausa. Africans, particularly in Nigeria, are producing excellent writers, whose books – written in English – are read throughout the English-speaking world. The following are all known internationally: Chinua Achebe, novelist, and Wole Soyinka, poet and dramatist, both of Nigeria; James Ngugi, Kenyan novelist; Amos Tutuola, a great Nigerian storyteller and very readable. Soyinka won the Nobel Prize for Literature in 1986.

> Chinua Achebe, the West African novelist, said in 1965 "I've been given this language and I intend to use it".
> Tony Fairman, *English Today* 7 July 86

The people of Senegal, Benin, Ivory Coast and other ex-French colonies still speak French. Ever since the 18th century, when French was the lingua franca* of Europe, the French have been jealous of the competition of English, which is the language of the Commonwealth. At Commonwealth meetings, English is the only common language. English is valuable, too, at Pan-African meetings.

In East Africa a completely different, non-European language has been the lingua franca of Africans for many

lingua franca common language

centuries. This is Swahili, which is a mixture of Arabic and African languages. The word 'swahili' comes from the Arabic word 'sawahili', meaning 'of the coast'. Swahili is used as the lingua franca of Kenya and Tanzania. The Portuguese traded on the East African coast for 200 years, but added no Portuguese words to Swahili.

During the great colonial drive of the late 19th century, each European power introduced its own language as the official language of its new colonies. But even where English is not the official language, it has remained an important link between people who speak different languages. The leaders and most members of the governments speak it fluently.

Swahili, which all British officials in East Africa had to learn, has some strange grammatical rules. For example, 'mtu' = 'person', but in the plural this becomes 'wa-tu' = 'people'. All the other words then begin with 'm-/ma-' or 'w-/wa-'. 'Wa-tu w-etu wa-le wa-kubwa wa-mekiya', which means 'those big people of ours have come'. Swahili has borrowed a number of words from English. For example, 'a traffic island' has become 'kiplefiti' (from 'keep left'), but the plural, 'traffic islands', obeys Swahili grammar. Singular words which begin with *ki* begin in the plural with *vi*, so 'viplefiti' is the plural of 'kiplefiti'.

English and Afrikaans are the official languages of South Africa. South African English has a slight Afrikaans accent, but is otherwise like standard English. A few Afrikaans words have found a place in the Oxford English Dictionary. 'Trek' is used throughout the English-speaking world. Most of the Cape coloureds (people who are not whites or Africans) speak English. The Africans, who are known as the 'Bantu' by South Africans, speak Zulu, Xhosa or one or more other African languages as well as English and/or Afrikaans.

African languages have given very few words to European languages. On the other hand, since many Africans now live in closer contact with the European style of life, they have had to find words for common objects and common verbs. For example in the Kxoe language of South West Africa, they call a watch 'ammuxo' which translated means 'sun-see-on-thing', and 'kuru' is used for 'drive' (a car), which translated means to 'press the bellows'. In Kxoe there are words for one, two, three, but after that they have to use images. For example, 'four' is 'the finger with which one licks out the pot'.

Swahili numbers

1	2	3	4	5	6	7	8	9	10
Moja	Mbili	Tatu	Nne	Tano	Sita	Saba	Nane	Tisa	Kumi

A   Vocabulary

1   Name one or two things you could call *local*.
2   How would you explain *English is the official language*?
3   How else could you say *a wide variety*?
4   What would you expect to find in a *journal*?
5   Give some examples of being *jealous*.
6   What does *common* mean in the phrase *common language*? There is another phrase which has the same meaning. What is it?
7   What is a *grammatical rule*?

B   Questions

1   Why is English often helpful to Nigerians when they meet other Nigerians?
2   What is the lingua franca of Northern Nigeria?
3   How do you know the African writers mentioned are having a great success?
4   Why did British colonial officials in East and Central Africa have to learn Swahili?
5   Which was the mother tongue (language) from which Afrikaans, the language of the Afrikaners, developed?

bellows they blow air into a fire to make it burn better

C   Grammar

Rewrite the following passage using contracted (short) forms: I wasn't, he didn't, I've etc.

I have met some strange people in my life, but nobody as strange as the man I met at Nairobi airport the other day. I do not know what his origin was. He was not black and he was not white, and he was not brown either. We were standing next to each other in the customs hall. He said, 'You are thinking I am not a Kenyan, are you not? Well, you are wrong, I have a Kenyan passport and I am hoping that they will let me in this time. They were not at all friendly last time. They called me an ivory poacher. "Ivory poacher! You are kidding," I said to them. "Of course I am not an ivory poacher!" Anyway, they said I would have to spend the night in a police cell!'

I had just picked up my suitcases when I stopped and asked him, 'Why are you here?'

'Ssh!' he said. 'I really am an ivory poacher!'

D   Function

Anger and regret

Make a list of all the words, phrases and sentences you know expressing 1) anger 2) regret 3) excuses. Then make up a dialogue between a boy and his girlfriend. He has kept her waiting for half an hour in the rain and she is wet and angry. They were going to see some African dancers. Now they've missed the beginning of the show. He says he had to wait hours for a bus. She says she doesn't believe his story—he's just not interested in African dancing ... etc. Make the dialogue as full as possible.